RACE, RIOTS,
AND THE
POLICE

Howard Rahtz

LYNNE
RIENNER
PUBLISHERS

BOULDER
LONDON

Published in the United States of America in 2016 by
Lynne Rienner Publishers, Inc.
1800 30th Street, Boulder, Colorado 80301
www.rienner.com

and in the United Kingdom by
Lynne Rienner Publishers, Inc.
3 Henrietta Street, Covent Garden, London WC2E 8LU

Library of Congress Cataloging-in-Publication Data
Names: Rahtz, Howard, author.
Title: Race, riots, and the police / by Howard Rahtz.
Description: Boulder, Colorado : Lynne Rienner Publishers, Inc., [2016] |
    Includes bibliographical references and index.
Identifiers: LCCN 2016016380 |
    ISBN 9781626375574 (hardcover : alk. paper) |
    ISBN 9781626375581 (pbk. : alk. paper)
Subjects: LCSH: Race riots—United States. | Police–community relations—
    United States. | Police brutality—United States. | United States—Race relations.
Classification: LCC HV6477 .R34 2016 | DDC 363.32/308900973—dc23
LC record available at https://lccn.loc.gov/2016016380

British Cataloguing in Publication Data
A Cataloguing in Publication record for this book
is available from the British Library.

Printed and bound in the United States of America

The paper used in this publication meets the requirements
of the American National Standard for Permanence of
Paper for Printed Library Materials Z39.48-1992.

5 4 3 2 1

Race, Riots,
and the Police

Contents

1

Race, Riots, and the Police

The black-white rift stands at the very center of American history. It is the great challenge to which all our deepest aspirations to freedom must rise . . . we forget who we are, and we make the great rift deeper and wider.

—Ken Burns, filmmaker

The fissure between the police and the African American community remains a major challenge for US society. Race-related riots, the violent manifestation of that rift, are one of the most devastating events that occur in a community, leaving deaths and injuries, economic damage, heightened racial tension, and increased crime in the aftermath.

Race relations is a complicated collection of issues that touch on virtually every aspect of American life. When race relations explode into rioting, police action will almost certainly be the spark.

The particular elements leading to racial violence have changed over the years. While race riots occur in the context of a convoluted mix of social, economic, and cultural factors, policing consistently remains a crucial piece of the equation. It would be overreaching to designate police action as the sole factor in race riots; nevertheless, the importance of the police in preventing and effectively responding when disorder occurs can hardly be overstated.

Race riots are nearly as old as the country itself. As a starting point for understanding the police role in these events, it is necessary to go back nearly 100 years. In 1919, race riots broke out in a number of cities around the country. That time became known as the Red Summer due to the widespread and violent nature of the riots—which were characterized largely by white mobs attacking the black community, while police either stood aside or in some cases acted in collusion with white rioters. In Chapter 2, I discuss the Red Summer riots in Chicago, Washington, DC, and Elaine, Arkansas. This was a period of particularly virulent racial animosity, when hundreds of black Americans were lynched by mobs and the Ku Klux Klan was in its ascendancy.

Chapter 2 also reviews the wave of widespread racial violence that occurred in 1943. Riots in a number of cities that year were particularly lethal, resulting in significant death tolls and injuries. The riots of 1943, in the midst of World War II, proved an embarrassment for the country and provided a propaganda boost for Nazi Germany. They also represented something of a transition in riot dynamics, offering significant lessons for modern police leaders.

In Chapter 3, I turn to review race rioting from the 1960s to 2015. After World War II, large-scale, race-related violence dissipated until the 1960s. That decade became one of the most turbulent periods in race relations in the country as the civil rights movement directly challenged the racial status quo. Between 1964 and 1971, there were more than 750 riots in the country, with a large number of these following the assassination of Dr. Martin Luther King Jr. in 1968 (Postrell 2004). While racial inequality in every facet of American life was challenged by Dr. King and the civil rights movement, policing in African American communities became a significant issue in the rioting.

The post-1960s disturbances moved policing to the predominant issue in race riots. The 1992 riot in Los Angeles, stemming from the acquittal of the LAPD police officers accused in the beating of Rodney King, was one of the most violent episodes of racial violence in our history. The news media took a central role in the King episode, with the beating and the racial attacks in South Central Los Angeles a year later captured on videotape and shown literally thousands of times on television.

At the turn of the century, police were once more the focal point of rioting. In Cincinnati in 2001, Oakland in 2009, Ferguson in 2014, and Baltimore in 2015, African American men dying at the hands of police officers led to disorder and exposed the fractured relationship between police and the black community.

Chapter 4 provides an overview of lessons drawn from the history of racial conflict. Each past episode of rioting provided guideposts to prevent future occurrences, and a review of the history of American race riots reads as a litany of squandered opportunities.

The priority lesson of riot history is the necessity for substantial steps by police leaders directly addressing the relationship between their departments and African American citizens. Although action to improve community trust is a priority, planning for disorder must not be ignored. Nearly every episode of rioting reviewed here included disorganized and sometimes chaotic government and police response, allowing disorder to persist and intensify.

If racism remains a spear pointed at the heart of America, police use of force is surely the tip. The intersection of race and police use of force is the flashpoint for racial conflagration, and Chapter 5 reviews the complicated issue of police use of force. The chapter covers the legal boundaries for police use of force, the effectiveness of force tools available to police, the role of race in police use of force, and a review of strategies to minimize police force incidents.

The nearly fifty-year war on drugs has been a major factor in the damaged relationship between African Americans and the police. Michelle Alexander, author of the acclaimed book *The New Jim Crow*, refers to the war on drugs as the "machine of mass incarceration." Chapter 6 reviews the racist underpinnings of the war on drugs, from the earliest drug laws to the explosion of incarceration as a result of modern drug enforcement. The chapter examines both the growth of police militarization and the erosion of constitutional protections stemming from drug enforcement.

In discussions of repairing the relationship between the police and African Americans, community-oriented policing (COP) is frequently proposed. COP as a policy was a linchpin of the presidency of Bill Clinton with his campaign promise of 100,000 new police officers added to the country's crime fighting effort. The promise of COP was the utilization of these new police officers as partners with the community in solving crime and disorder problems.

In Chapter 7, a brief history of COP is reviewed with an examination of its potential to bridge the gap between police and the community. The concept of police legitimacy is introduced as a key factor in the process, and the synergy possible between COP and efforts to promote legitimacy is described.

Police legitimacy is a crucial concept in improving police and community relations. In Chapter 8, the dimensions of the challenge are outlined in a review of survey data measuring the depth of the gap between African Americans and the police. Analysis of steps taken by corporate entities to strengthen brand equity, a challenge analogous to improving police legitimacy, provide a starting point for discussion of police organizational strategies to enhance legitimacy. Community engagement efforts by both individual police officers and their departments are crucial steps to build legitimacy, and a number of examples are provided. The role of social media in development of the community engagement effort is also discussed.

Chapter 9 outlines the use of community forums as a strategy to jump-start efforts at community engagement. Discussion of race relations remains an uncomfortable conversation in modern-day America, and the related topic of tension between the police and the African American community is infrequently discussed in an open fashion. However, the potential for improved trust and respect begins with these conversations.

There are a number of specific policy steps for local and state governments that will enhance community engagement. Chapter 10 explores some of these options. An issue coming out of the current focus on police-related deaths is the lack of national data on force incidents. Media stories have highlighted the fact that police-related deaths are not captured by any current reporting system, leaving leaders struggling with a problem for which accurate data does not exist.

The chapter also focuses on use of state authority in certifying police officers. While nearly all states set specific standards for certification as a police officer, the state power to decertify police officers guilty of official misconduct or criminal behavior is rarely employed. The process proposed follows the model used by state bar associations or state medical associations in disciplining members of those professions.

Chapter 11 details several specific steps for police that could contribute to lowering the tension with the communities they serve. The challenge for today's police leaders is to forge relationships with their communities that replace fear and distrust with respect and cooperation. For police officers, the failures of the past become the burden of the present. With policing front and center as the primary issue in US race relations, the current focus on police reform represents an opportunity for courageous and creative action by police and community leaders to finally move forward in closing the racial divide.

2

From the Red
Summer to 1943

Discrimination in arrest was a principal cause of widespread and long-standing distrust. Whether justified or not, this feeling was actual and bitter.
—Chicago Commission on Race Relations (1922)

The upholding of a white, Klan-led mob, who refused to let Negroes use the streets of this free country, not only has left . . . the Detroit Police Department . . . and Mayor Jeffries in disgrace but has branded these men as unfit to be classed as believers in law and order.

—Detroit Tribune (1942)

Riots in the summer of 1919 broke out in more than thirty cities, including Knoxville, Omaha, New York, Syracuse, and Baltimore. Some of the worst rioting occurred in Chicago, Washington, DC, and Elaine, Arkansas. The rioting exposed the racial tension of the period, and a review of the riots in Chicago, Washington, and Elaine provides a glimpse of the social factors and the role of the police.

The Red Summer of 1919: Chicago

On July 27, 1919, Chicago was sweltering under both a heat wave and escalating racial tension. In the weeks prior, there had been a number of white gang assaults on black residents. Just five weeks earlier, two black Chicagoans, each walking alone on the border between black and white neighborhoods, had been brutally murdered by white gangs. Threats of violence by both blacks and whites on at least two occasions in the days prior to July 27 led the Chicago Police Department to flood the area between white and black neighborhoods with officers in an effort to deter trouble.

Chicago beaches were packed on July 27. The unofficial barrier between white and black beachgoers was 29th Street and its imaginary line continuing into Lake Michigan. On the afternoon of July 27, four black men entered the white side of the beach and were immediately greeted by some of the whites throwing stones. The four men left the area but returned shortly with reinforcements, and rock throwing between groups of blacks and whites ensued. Eugene Williams, a seventeen-year-old African American, had entered the water on the black section of the beach but then drifted onto the white side as the rock fight escalated. As rocks began to fall around him, he grabbed onto a floating railroad tie for support. As one white youth swam toward Williams, he let go of the railroad tie and disappeared under the water.[1]

Williams's apparent drowning had a temporary sobering effect on both groups. Whites and blacks dove into the water in a vain attempt to rescue him. When a Chicago policeman arrived on the scene, the uneasy truce ended. Blacks pointed to a white man and identified him as the one whose rock had struck Williams. The crowd demanded the white man's arrest. The officer refused. Word began to spread that the officer had refused to arrest Williams's murderer, and anger began to grow. As the crowd seethed, an officer began to arrest one of the black men. Some members of the crowd immediately attacked the officer. As other officers responded, a black man, James Crawford, fired a gun at the officers. One of the officers returned fire, killing Crawford, and the riot was under way.[2]

Within two hours, rioting and fighting was in full swing. Over the next few days, blacks were pulled off streetcars and beaten. Whites traversing through black neighborhoods were assaulted by angry crowds. Groups of whites burned black businesses and residences, eventually leaving thousands homeless. The rioting raged for seven days, ending only when authorities deployed the state militia. More than 500 people were injured in the rioting, and 38 people were killed (Chicago Commission on Race Relations 1922).

Red Summer: Washington, DC

In 1919, a week prior to the rioting in Chicago, Washington, DC exploded. The flashpoint was not an identifiable event as in Chicago but resulted from an environment of racial animus driven in part by an irresponsible media.

In the weeks prior to the Washington riot, local newspapers had published an unrelenting series of articles focused on a "Negro fiend" attacking white women. There were four daily newspapers in Washington, and the headlines from July of 1919 fueled a mob mentality. The headlines included "13 Suspects Arrested in Negro Hunt," "Posses Keep Up Hunt For Negro," and "Negro Fiend Sought Anew" (Perl 1999).

On July 19, in a section of town known as Murder Bay, crowds of marines, sailors, and soldiers on leave were packed into the area's bars and brothels. When the rumor that a black man accused of sexual assault on a white woman (the wife of a sailor) had been released by the police, an angry crowd moved from Murder Bay across the National Mall toward the southwest section of the city. The crowd assaulted blacks they encountered, beating them with sticks and pipes. Police responded slowly, but as officers arrived, they began to arrest more blacks than whites.

After that first night, what might have ended as a minor racial skirmish escalated at least partly because of media encouragement. That morning, the *Washington Post* published a front-page article with the headline "Mobilization for Tonight," announcing that all available servicemen were to report to Pennsylvania and 7th for a "clean-up" operation. The so-called mobilization was bogus, but the damage was done (Perl 1999).

The black community, realizing that city authorities would not provide protection, began arming themselves for defense of their neighborhood. An estimated 500 guns were purchased that day in neighborhood pawnshops. Black Army veterans, armed with rifles, took up rooftop positions, and barricades were set up on major thoroughfares (Perl 1999).

That night, crowds of blacks and whites gathered. Both groups engaged in drive-by shootings and assaults targeting those of the other race. At the end of the night, fifteen were dead, including one police officer.

The next day, with the situation clearly out of control, President Woodrow Wilson mobilized troops to stop the rioting. City leaders closed saloons and businesses in the areas victimized by the rioting. Despite the presence of the troops, white mobs gathered, and more violence appeared likely. A torrential downpour that lasted through the night dispersed the mobs. The weather, together with the troop presence, effectively ended the rioting.

Red Summer: Elaine

The 1919 riot in Elaine, Arkansas, was different from Chicago and Washington. Elaine was a largely rural area and majority African American. Factors in the rioting included racial hatred and fear of organized labor and communist influences. The aftermath of the riot also highlighted abuses in the criminal justice system as local authorities zealously prosecuted blacks alleged to have been involved in the shooting that instigated the rioting.

On the night of September 30, about a hundred black farmers were meeting at a church with officials of the Progressive Farmer's and Household Union. The purpose of the meeting was organizing the farmers to push for higher wages from white landowners. Anticipating trouble, meeting organizers posted armed guards outside the church. A car pulled up in front of the church, and gunfire erupted between the guards and three individuals in the car. Exactly how and why the gunfight began is in dispute, but at the end of the firing one man in the car was dead, and another was wounded. The dead man was W. A. Adkins, a white security officer from the Missouri-Pacific Railroad. The wounded man was a white Phillips County deputy sheriff, Charles Pratt.

The next day, the sheriff organized a posse to arrest the blacks believed responsible for shooting Adkins and Pratt. Spurred by rumors of a Negro "insurrection," some 500 to 1,000 white men, some local and some crossing the river from nearby Mississippi, joined the posse. Descending on the black community and facing minimal resistance, the posse reportedly killed an unknown number of black citizens and arrested hundreds of others, placing them in makeshift stockades. County authorities, perhaps stunned by the intensity of the violence, made repeated requests to the state for help. The next day, at the request of the governor, 500 federal troops were dispatched to Elaine. With the arrival of the troops on October 2, the white mob dispersed, but the violence continued as troops assaulted and killed blacks. The commander of the troops, Colonel Isaac Jenks, reported only two Negroes killed by the troops, but other observers put the number much higher. Sharpe Dunaway, an employee of the *Arkansas Gazette*, testified in 1925 the soldiers "committed one murder after another with all the calm deliberation in the world, either too heartless to realize the enormity of their crimes, or too drunk on moonshine to give a continental dam" (Stockley n.d.)

Discussion

The Red Summer is nearly a century past, but the events of that year echo in current conversations on race and policing. Although it is clear that the police engaged in racist practices, their actions were consistent with the racial attitudes of that era. The early decades of the twentieth century were characterized by some of the most virulent racism in the country's history. The Ku Klux Klan was in its ascendancy and active as a social and political force. Lynching of African Americans in the twenty years prior to 1919 totaled nearly 1,500 people (Archives of the Tuskegee Institue n.d.) White and black societies were almost entirely separate, and blacks suffered discrimination in every aspect of social life.

Race riots prior to 1919 had largely followed a common script. A rumor of a black man attacking a white man or woman was followed by mobs of white men descending on black neighborhoods, physically assaulting people and burning their homes while police stood by.

By 1919, that script had begun to change. The Red Summer riot in Chicago was unusual as one of the first instances of rioting not generated by such a rumor. The migration of thousands of African Americans to Chicago during the early years of the century had begun to change the city's racial dynamics. Wartime labor shortages contributed to the influx of African Americans into the city and into employment in the defense industry. Chicago was also the site of large contingents of both white and black service members in the country's then segregated military. African Americans who had fought in Europe during World War I were increasingly dissatisfied with the racial status quo. Crowded housing, food shortages, a repressive police presence, and a hostile white community all contributed to the escalating racial tensions.

In light of the widespread racial enmity in Chicago, perhaps it is not surprising that these tensions were most acute along the rigid lines of segregation at a public beach. In such a highly charged atmosphere, the perceived racist action by the police at the scene of Williams's drowning was the match to the racial tinderbox.

In the 1919 riot in Washington, many of the same elements that existed in Chicago were also present. Crowded housing and lack of jobs in the postwar economy were particularly acute, and it was a common sight to see returning veterans, white and black, in uniform, panhandling on the streets. Compared with Chicago, Washington's black community was prosperous, with a growing middle class of lawyers, ministers, teachers, and businesspeople. The movement of middle-class African Americans into previously all-white neighborhoods added to the local racial tension.

Washington was also home to thousands of returning black war veterans who believed, like their counterparts in Chicago, that their military service would lead to fairer treatment in society. African Americans were hopeful the election of President Woodrow Wilson, who had promised a "new freedom" and won the majority of black votes, would lead to change. But Wilson brought with him a conservative administration intent on imposing a Jim Crow system imported from the South. Facilities in government agencies had been somewhat integrated, but Wilson's regime rolled back the move toward integration and established Jim Crow corners with separate restrooms and eating areas.

The initial impetus for the Washington rioting—a rumor of a black man attacking a white woman—was a theme that had instigated many of the US riots prior to 1919. But in Washington, the role of the media in fanning the flames of racial hatred through reckless reporting of alleged black attacks on whites was particularly notable. The Washington chapter of the National Association for the Advancement of Colored People (NAACP) was so concerned with the inflammatory nature of the media they sent a warning letter to the city's four daily papers. These letters, sent just a few weeks prior to the riot, noted the incendiary nature of the headlines was "sowing the seeds of a race riot" (Perl 1999).

The Elaine riot also marked a departure from previous racial violence. While the shooting at the church generated the spark, the tinder included the fear of black farmers joining labor unions. Furthermore, while a few authorities in Chicago and Washington claimed the presence of outside agitators as factors in the rioting, Elaine authorities embraced the narrative of a "Negro insurrection" and plot to kill white people. Union members and communists were blamed for instigating the alleged black rebellion.

While authorities in Chicago and Washington failed to protect black communities, by some accounts, authorities in Elaine were complicit in the murder of an unknown number of their African American citizens. Mobs of white men, acting under the color of law as members of a posse, reportedly killed hundreds of African Americans. Unfortunately, the killing did not stop with the arrival of military troops (Stockey n.d.).

Postriot actions also played out differently. In Chicago, a study group, the Chicago Commission of Race Relations, established with the support of the mayor and the governor of Illinois, produced a comprehensive report detailing both the riot and the social conditions contributing to it. That report, *The Negro in Chicago: A Study of Race Relations and a Race Riot*, is striking for its unflinching look at the 1919 rioting.

In Washington, attempts by the NAACP and other groups to review the rioting were blocked by federal authorities. However, the Washington riot galvanized the black community as never before. The riot in 1919 marked one of the first occasions where the black community organized to defend itself. Sociologist Arthur Waqskow, interviewing survivors, noted that the experience had provided them with a new self-respect and a "readiness to face white society as equals" (Perl 1999).

The aftermath of the Elaine riot was notable for the corruption of the criminal justice system in prosecuting black suspects. Authorities convened a Committee of Seven charged with investigating the causes of the rioting. The committee was made up entirely of prominent white citizens of Phillips County. After meeting with the committee, Hillman Brough, the governor of Arkansas, announced "The situation at Elaine has been well handled and is absolutely under control. . . . The white citizens of the county deserve unstinting praise for their actions in preventing mob violence" (Stockey n.d.).

Postriot actions by the authorities in Elaine remain a study on race-based suppression. Although the role of whites in the violence was ignored, black residents of Elaine paid a heavy price. Authorities justified their actions on the rationale they had been facing a black revolt and insisted the repressive actions of the police and military had prevented a murderous attack on the white community. The Committee of Seven concluded the violence was a "black rebellion." One local leader told a *Helena World* reporter, "The present trouble with the Negroes in Phillips County is not a race riot. It is a deliberately planned insurrection of the Negroes against the whites directed by an organization known as the 'Progressive Farmers and Household Union of America,' established for the purpose of banding Negroes together for the killing of white people" (Stockey n.d.).

It was left to the national office of the NAACP to dispute that conclusion. The NAACP dispatched a representative, Walter White, to investigate the Elaine riots. White concluded the alleged Negro insurrection was "only a figment of the imagination of Arkansas whites and not based on fact" (Stockey n.d.).

The African Americans arrested in the Elaine rioting faced severe consequences. Although the exact number is unknown, hundreds of blacks were detained in temporary stockades during the rioting. Some were released after being vouched for by white employers. Somewhere between 200 and 300 others were moved to the county jail in Helena. The jail's reported capacity was forty-eight prisoners. On October 31, 1919, a county grand jury returned indictments against 122 African American men, with charges ranging from homicide to terroristic threatening.

The first twelve defendants, all charged with murder, were tried the following week. Local white attorneys were appointed to represent the men. Quickly, all-white juries found the men guilty, and Judge J. M. Jackson sentenced all of them to death in the electric chair. Seeing the writing on the wall, sixty-five others pleaded guilty to second-degree murder and were given lengthy jail sentences.

If not for the efforts of the NAACP, the sentences of these men would have stood. A notable black attorney, Scorpio Jones, with the support of the NAACP, took up the appeals for the initial group of defendants, who came to be known as the Elaine 12. Jones was joined in his effort by a white lawyer, a man named George C. Murphy, who was a well-known politician in Arkansas, had served as state attorney general, and had also run for governor. Murphy, age seventy-nine at the time of the trial, was a former Confederate Army officer and was viewed as one of the most effective trial lawyers in the state. After a five-year legal battle, Jones and Murphy were successful in having many of the original convictions overturned.

Tulsa, 1921

Race-related violence did not disappear after the Red Summer of 1919. A history of race rioting of that era would be incomplete without mention of the Greenwood riot in Tulsa, Oklahoma, in 1921.

In 1921, Tulsa was a thriving and growing city. Its population was about 100,000, which included an estimated 10,000 African Americans living in the Greenwood area. Greenwood was a vibrant community, including theaters, restaurants, churches, community newspapers, a library, and a multitude of other black-owned businesses.

Like much of the racial violence in that era, the rioting began with rumor of a sexual assault on a white woman. Sarah Page was an elevator operator in the Drexel Building in downtown Tulsa. Dick Rowland, an African American, worked shining shoes in the same building (Ellsworth n.d.). On May 30, Rowland entered the elevator operated by Page. Exactly what occurred is unknown, but most authorities believe Rowland tripped as he entered the elevator, falling against or stepping on the foot of Page, who screamed. A worker in the building heard the scream and saw Rowland flee the building. That person called authorities and reported the assault. Rowland was arrested the next day.

Shortly after word of his arrest spread through the community, a group of whites gathered at the courthouse, demanding the sheriff turn Rowland over to the crowd. Hearing rumors of the crowd and determined to prevent Rowland's lynching, about twenty-five armed African American men sped to the courthouse and met with the sheriff, offering help in protecting Rowland from the crowd. The sheriff declined, stating he was in control of the situation, and he advised the group to return to Greenwood.

As the day wore on, the crowd at the courthouse grew, and rumors reached Greenwood of a white mob attacking the local National Guard Armory and taking weapons. With concern over the possible lynching of Rowland growing, a larger contingent of about seventy-five armed African Americans went again to the courthouse to meet with the sheriff. The sheriff once again declined their help, re-stating he had control of the situation and advising them to return to Greenwood. As the group left the courthouse, one of the white men in the crowd confronted one of the African Americans, demanding that he turn over his weapon. A fight broke out, a shot was fired, and the riot was on.

The African American group retreated to Greenwood, exchanging gunfire with the crowd of whites following. By the early morning of June 1, a white mob was setting fires on the outskirts of Greenwood. At dawn the mob moved into Greenwood and burned the community to the ground. An estimated 300 African Americans were killed in the violence, and the majority of the Greenwood residents fled the area.

As in Elaine, authorities were complicit in the violence. Members of the mob at the courthouse were deputized and took part in the burning of Greenwood. The state militia was called in but did not intervene in the violence and was instead deployed to protect white neighborhoods from a rumored attack.

Rowland remained in the county jail until September 1921, when Sarah Page wrote a letter to the sheriff indicating she did not want to pursue any charges. Following his release, Rowland left Tulsa and dropped out of sight. A complete accounting of the Greenwood riot did not occur until 2001 (Oklahoma Commission 2001).

Following the Greenwood riot, there were periodic outbreaks of race-related violence, but the next outbreak of widespread rioting occurred in 1943.

The Race Riots of 1943: Detroit

Detroit, New York, Los Angeles, Mobile, Philadelphia, Indianapolis, Baltimore, and St. Louis were all sites of race riots in 1943. A review of the riots in a few of these cities highlights the context of race in the United States during World War II and also illustrates some social dynamics with continuing relevance. Certainly, the role of the police prior to and during the rioting provides continuing lessons.

The 1943 riot in Detroit began on the evening of June 20. The day was swelteringly hot, and white and black residents of Detroit crowded Belle Isle, a popular recreation area with beaches and picnic areas. A group of blacks, intent on revenge for the beating of African Americans in the week before, jumped a white pedestrian. The white man ran to a nearby naval armory seeking help, and a group of sailors ran out to confront the blacks.

A large brawl ensued, spreading quickly to the mainland side of the bridge, where white mobs began to attack blacks caught in the area. By 2 a.m., the fighting had begun to die down but reignited as rumors swept through the crowds. One rumor had a man bursting into a crowded bar and announcing that a white mob had killed a black woman and her baby by throwing them off the Belle Isle bridge. The crowd surged out of the bar, seeking vengeance (Jackman 2003).

On the predominantly black east side of Detroit, crowds began to attack whites driving through the area. Police in riot gear were mobilized, and what Michael Jackman refers to as a "police riot" erupted.

Police discharged live ammunition to disperse crowds and shot those who had begun looting the neighborhood stores.

By early Monday morning, the same rumor that had earlier incited a black crowd circulated among the white mob. The rumor was that a black man had tossed a white woman off the bridge. The rumor quickly morphed to a pregnant woman being thrown off the bridge and then morphed again to a woman and her baby thrown off the bridge.

Whatever the motivation, a crowd of whites gathered on Woodward Avenue and began attacking blacks leaving the street's all-night theaters. As the morning broke, the mob grew and blacks going to work on streetcars were pulled off and beaten. Outnumbered or indifferent, the police took little action.

As the day wore on, the violence escalated. The size of the white mob increased, and it began to move relentlessly east toward the ghetto. As city authorities debated on the appropriate response, violence broke out just outside City Hall. After witnessing a crowd of whites chase and beat a black man, the decision was made to declare martial law and call in federal troops (Jackman 2003). Prior to the troops' arrival, pleas for calm from the mayor and black ministers were ignored.

On June 21, some twenty-four hours after the riot started, the troops arrived and managed to get control of the streets. The death tally was thirty-four, with hundreds more injured and millions in property damage.

Race Riots of 1943: Los Angeles

The Los Angeles riot in 1943 was different in some aspects than the other race-related rioting that summer. The violence was not between whites and blacks but primarily between whites and Latinos. The violence came to be called the zoot suit riots, after the distinctive clothing worn by young Latinos known as pachucos.

Media activity played a role in the LA violence. In the middle of World War II, with the United States in a bloody conflict with the Japanese, LA papers regularly described Latinos as a race of "Oriental persuasion" (Baeder 2013). The so-called Oriental connection linked the pachucos with Japanese Americans, who were being rounded up and forced into interment centers. Newspapers were characterized by biased and exaggerated coverage of pachuco violence against whites.

In the spring of 1943, media stories on Latinos included:

- "L.A. Zoot Suit Disorder Spreads: Pachuco Gangs Tangle in New Street Brawls With Navy; Cry 'Death to Cops'" (*Long Beach Independent*, June 1943)
- "Hobble Skirts Hide Razors: Zoot Suiters Run for Cover but Their 'Cholitas' Carry On" (*Washington Daily News*, June 1943)
- "Pachucos Origins Traced: Zoot Suit Is Symbol of Hatred of Society" (*Long Beach Independent*, June 1943)
- "Communists had Big Part in Zoot Suit Riots" (*Corona Daily Independent*, June 1943)
- "28 Zoot Suiters Seized on Coast after Clashes with Service Men" (*New York Times*, June 1943) (Baeder 2013).

A naval armory located in the middle of a Hispanic neighborhood became the epicenter of escalating violence between sailors and the zoot suiters. A fight between the two groups on May 30 resulted in serious injury to at least one sailor and the zoot suiters forced the sailors to retreat into the armory. The sailors plotted a revenge attack and on the night of June 3, about fifty sailors, armed with clubs, left the armory and began looking for young men in zoot suits to attack. After assaulting the victims, the sailors tore the offending clothes and burned them. On the second night, the sailors were joined by marines and other service members and moved into nearby Hispanic neighborhoods, entering bars and theaters, attacking those they encountered.

The police largely stood by. One officer explained the nonaction, noting, "Many of us were in the First World War, and we're not going to pick on kids in the service" (PBS n.d.). The rioting went on for nearly a week and only ended when the military declared Los Angeles off limits and servicemen were ordered to remain in their barracks.

Race Riots of 1943: Harlem

The 1943 riot in Harlem began as a routine police matter. On August 1, a police officer named James Collins was investigating a dispute between a porter at the Hotel Braddock and an African American customer, Margie Polite. Polite had secured a room at the hotel but then complained the room was not satisfactory. She was given another room, which she also found not to her liking, and demanded a refund.

Refund in hand, Polite was on her way out of the hotel when she encountered a porter to whom she had previously given a $1 tip. Since she was not staying at the hotel, she insisted the porter return her tip. He refused. The two began arguing and police were called. Collins, a white rookie officer, decided to arrest Polite. She resisted, and Collins began to physically restrain her.

In the hotel lobby and witnessing the altercation was Robert Bandy, an African American war veteran. Bandy was in the company of his mother. He objected to Collins's actions with Polite and physically intervened on her behalf, taking Collins's police baton away from the officer and striking him with it. Collins then shot Bandy, wounding him in the shoulder. Bandy was arrested and taken to a local hospital, suffering a minor wound.

Word of the incident quickly spread. As the story swirled through the neighborhood, the incident was cast as police brutality and Bandy was said to have been killed by the officer in front of his mother. Crowds quickly gathered at the hotel, the hospital where Bandy had been taken, and the local police precinct. As the crowds grew, they began to move through the neighborhood, breaking windows and looting businesses. The rioting lasted two days before being brought under control.

Police responded in force, flooding the neighborhood with more than 6,000 officers, 8,000 state guardsmen, and hundreds of volunteers. The volunteers included 300 black women who were deputized, provided police batons, and sent out to the streets as peacekeepers. As a result of the rioting, 500 people were arrested. Despite the significant property damage and large number of arrests, deaths were minimal, with five people killed by police. Forty officers suffered injuries in the melee.

Discussion

The 1943 Detroit violence, one of the most deadly riots in US history, looked much like the 1919 Red Summer riots. In 1943, the United State was in the middle of World War II, and a large number of African Americans had migrated to Detroit and were finding employment in the city's war industries. The poor social conditions, inadequate and crowded housing, wartime shortages, and a repressive police presence contributed to growing racial tension.

Both the Detroit rioting and Chicago's 1919 riots began at beach and recreation areas, where whites and blacks shared uneasy racial boundaries. Both riots were preceded by racial assaults, followed by escalating revenge attacks. Both riots were characterized by at best an indifferent police response, and by some accountings, police collusion with white rioters. The Detroit rioting was also notable for a large number of people killed and injured as large crowds of whites and blacks fought each other.

The role of the rumor mill in facilitating the violence in Detroit is noteworthy. Rumors ran unchecked. Retaliatory attacks by blacks and whites in response to rumors characterized much of the violence.

The 1943 Detroit rioting was a national embarrassment. Detroit was a crucial location in the war production effort, and race rioting not only disrupted that production but shone a bright light on the systemic racism in the country. That schism in US society and the resulting rioting provided a propaganda coup for Nazi Germany. The rioting was prominently featured in German media and Roosevelt had to divert troops from the front in North Africa to quell the rioting.

The zoot suit riot was distinctly different from the Red Summer rioting in that the target was Hispanics rather than African Americans. Although the racial component was different, the dynamics of the rioting were markedly similar. The role the media played in demonizing zoot suiters and characterizing them as "Oriental" was particularly powerful in the charged atmosphere following the Japanese attack on Pearl Harbor.

The LA zoot suit riots were also a notable example of military service members as primary actors. The presence of a large number of young white men, members of a segregated military, located in the middle of a Hispanic neighborhood, clearly contributed to racial tensions. Military service members were also prominently involved in the 1943 Detroit rioting and the 1919 Washington event.

Similar to the Detroit rioting, the police role in the zoot suit riots ranged from indifference to collusion. Only the central authority and power of the military structure prevented the situation from worsening. Once the service members were ordered to remain in their barracks, the rioting was essentially over.

The particular irritant of the zoot suits echoes somewhat in modern-day America. The present-day debate over baggy pants and tattoos as symbols for gang and criminal activity looks strikingly similar to the zoot suit controversy.

The Harlem riot of 1943 most clearly captures a transition in riot dynamics. Unlike previous incidents, the white population was not involved. Rather than pitched battles between whites and blacks, the anger of the black population was directed at police as well as shopkeepers and businesses perceived as exploiting the community. The race-based attacks so characteristic of earlier riots were absent.

Perhaps the most unique aspect of the Harlem riot response was the deputizing of black women from the community as peacekeepers. Although the authorities in 1943 would not have phrased it as such, the move conveyed recognition that law enforcers or peacekeepers identified with the community carry a legitimacy that police viewed as outsiders do not. The present debate about police diversity and community policing is a continuation of that 75-year-old notion.

The Harlem riot death toll was low. It is only speculation, but the potential reasons for that deserve mention. Authorities quickly deployed a massive presence to suppress the violence. More than 16,000 men, including police officers and national guard troops, were quickly deployed (City University of New York n.d.). While the neighborhood women represented only a small percentage of the peacekeepers, they likely had two effects. First, their presence may have restrained some of the brutality exhibited by police and guardsmen in other riot cities, and second, their presence as legitimate symbols of authority may have had a dampening impact on potential riot participants.

The precipitating incident in the Harlem riot also resonates in police tactics and behavior. Although there is little direct information on the dialogue among Collins, Polite, and Bandy, in the context of 1943 race relations, the situation was loaded with racial dynamite. What should have been a routine case of dispute resolution escalated into an attack on the officer and the subsequent shooting of Bandy.

Harlem in 1943 is another illustration of the power of the rumor. The belief that Bandy had been killed by the officer, in front of his mother, rocketed through the community and fueled the disorder. Bandy had in fact suffered a minor wound, but once the rioting began, the particulars of the incident mattered little.

As the country celebrated the end of World War II and moved into the 1950s, racial violence declined. In the 1960s, widespread rioting again struck the country and once again, policing was at the center of the violence.

Notes

1. Later autopsy results found no injuries to Williams that could be attributed to rocks.

2. The officer who killed Crawford was an African American, one of a handful of black officers on the Chicago Police Department in 1919.

3

From the 1960s to Baltimore

Burn, baby, burn! —Los Angeles, 1967

Hands up! —Ferguson, 2014

The decade of the 1960s was one of the most tempestuous times in US history. The civil rights struggle, the Vietnam War, the assassinations of President John Kennedy, his brother Robert Kennedy, and Martin Luther King Jr. all contributed to upheavals across the nation. Through the 1960s, the country experienced hundreds of incidents of racial rioting. Although the greatest number of these occurred in 1968 in the aftermath of King's assassination, the most violent riots happened in the years just prior to his death. Although King's murder was the clear flashpoint for the riots immediately following, the spark for others stemmed from the routine of police activity in racially tense ghettos.

The 1965 riot in Los Angeles and the 1967 riot in Newark were two of the most violent race riots of that time. The riots in these cities represented a marked change from previous incidents as police became the primary focus of the rioting. These riots were, in a very real sense, direct action against police using urban warfare tactics, including use of Molotov cocktails and snipers. A review of the precipitating incidents and police response to the riots carries continuing lessons for police leadership.

Los Angeles, 1965

In a decade where the expression "long, hot summer" took on new meaning, Los Angeles in August 1965 was ready to explode. On August 11, the temperature was over 90 degrees, and in neighborhoods simmering with tension between the police and residents, it took only a simple, routine action by a police officer to provide the spark.

At about 7:00 p.m. on August 11, California Highway Patrol Officer Lee Minikus pulled over a suspected drunk driver on Avalon Street, just outside the city limits of Los Angeles. The driver of the car was an African American, Marquette Frye. His brother was a passenger. With the odor of alcohol on Frye's breath, Minikus had him exit the car and move to the sidewalk. He then began to put Frye through street-side psychomotor tests. A crowd gathered to watch the encounter.

At the outset, the interaction between Frye and Minikus was friendly. Frye was animated in explaining he was definitely not drunk, and Minikus and the gathered crowd were amused by his antics. The atmosphere changed when Frye's mother, who lived nearby, arrived.

The mother was upset that Frye was intoxicated and much to the entertainment of the crowd began to loudly berate her son for his drunkenness. Upset with his mother, the crowd, and the police, Frye, according to Minikus, just "blew up" (Stahl n.d.). Screaming that the police would have to kill him, Frye ran into the crowd pursued by officers, and a fight ensued as the police tried to control and handcuff him. The crowd began turning hostile, and officers called for assistance.

Things worsened when Frye's mother and brother joined in the fight. The onlookers became angry when one of the officers struck Frye with his nightstick, causing a cut to his forehead. Officers finally got the family members under arrest. In less than thirty minutes from the initial stop, the crowd had grown from a handful of people to a group estimated in the hundreds.

What might have ended as a minor incident escalated when as the police began to leave the scene, someone in the crowd spit in an officer's face. In response, the police moved back into the crowd, arresting a woman for the spitting and a man for inciting the crowd. As the police pulled away from the scene, the crowd threw rocks and bottles at the squad car.

Rumors provided fuel for the rioting. The woman arrested for the spitting incident was wearing a smock that resembled maternity wear. Her arrest quickly morphed through the rumor mill as police abuse of a pregnant woman.

The police pulled out from the area, and the rioting began. The crowd began to stop and assault white motorists passing through, and looting of area businesses began. The first night, rioting was limited largely to the immediate area of the arrest. By the early morning hours, conditions had calmed down, and government and police officials began efforts to de-escalate the situation.

Later that day, community leaders and local officials organized a meeting at a local church in an attempt to forestall further rioting. Police officials, clergy, and others, including Frye's mother, addressed the crowd, imploring people to stay home. But the meeting broke down when an emotional neighborhood resident took the microphone and suggested attacking white people. Those comments became the focal point of widespread news coverage, and police and government representatives left the meeting to begin preparing for what everyone believed would be a resumption of rioting.

Thursday evening, crowds gathered near the location of the original arrest, and rioting resumed with multiple fires set and crowds looting stores. The police set up a perimeter around the area and attempted to contain it, but rioting began to spread to other areas of the city. When fire companies responded, they were greeted with rocks and bottles, which quickly escalated to sniper fire.

The National Guard was deployed around 11 p.m. Thursday night, but despite their presence, on Friday morning at 8 a.m., crowds began to re-form, and shortly thereafter rioting was in full swing. Rioting eventually encompassed a forty-six-square-mile area, and over 100 fire companies were responding to calls that came in every few minutes. Fire fighters were forced to operate under the threat of gunfire, and that night a firefighter was killed when a burning building collapsed on him. Also on Friday night, a county deputy was murdered while struggling with a man over a shotgun.

A curfew was imposed on Saturday, which had a dampening effect on the rioting. It took two more days before full control was established. Thirty-four people were killed in the rioting. Over 1,000 injuries were reported, with more than 100 of those resulting from gunfire. More than 600 buildings were damaged by fire, and the total property damage resulting from the riot was estimated at $40 million.

Newark, 1967

Like most of the United States in the summer of 1967, the city of Newark was seething with racial tension. What started as a police traffic stop around 9:45 the evening of July 12 resulted in rioting which rocked Newark for seven days.

The incident began when John Smith, a cab driver, pulled around a stopped police car. Officers Vito Pontrelli and John DeSimone stopped Smith for a tailgating violation. The stop quickly went bad. Police accounts of the incident say Smith struck the officers when told he was under arrest. He was put in the patrol car and taken to the Fourth Precinct station. On arrival, Smith was carried out of the police car into the police station. Again, the police account and Smith's account differ, with police claiming he refused to walk into the station and Smith stating he had been beaten and was unable to walk.

The Fourth Precinct was directly across from a large public housing project, and witnesses to Smith's arrest and forcible carry into the police station called local civil rights activists to report the situation. The network of black cab drivers spread the word of the arrest, and cabs and drivers descended on the police station, joining a growing crowd protesting Smith's arrest. Local leaders, including Robert Curvin from CORE (Congress of Racial Equality), showed up at the station and demanded to see Smith. Curvin and two others were taken into the station and observed that Smith appeared to have been beaten; they insisted that Smith be taken to the hospital immediately. The police complied.

By 11 p.m., the crowd outside the station had grown. The police requested that Curvin speak to the growing crowd and ask them to disperse. With a bullhorn provided by the police, Curvin pleaded with the crowd to disperse. His request was ignored, and some began breaking windows at the police station. In short order, a Molotov cocktail was thrown at the station, the crowd began to break windows in local business establishments, and rioting engulfed the area.

The next morning, a Thursday, Mayor Hugh Addonizio announced the incidents had not been a riot and had been contained by the police. Despite the pronouncement, early Thursday evening, crowds gathered again, looting ensued, and the police were quickly overwhelmed.

The first death of the riot occurred when police killed a looter early Friday morning; by daybreak, five people had been killed and hundreds more injured. Throughout the day Friday, the National Guard was deployed along with the police, but their combined efforts were unable to suppress the rioting, which continued for three more days. By the time the rioting died out, twenty-six people were dead, hundreds more were injured, and property damage exceeded $10 million.

Discussion

The race riots in the 1960s, particularly in Newark and Los Angeles, were no longer characterized by a passive black population under siege by white mobs while police were largely indifferent. The 1960s riots were more a direct attack on the police as symbols of white authority. Unlike the riots twenty years earlier, when white and black crowds directly fought each other, in Newark and Los Angeles, the police became the focal point of the violence. Police were targets of rocks and bottles and were facing Molotov cocktails thrown at squad cars and police positions. Gunfire directed at the police was a new challenge for the authorities, and shooters firing from ghetto rooftops and buildings brought a new lethality to the rioting. At times, the gun battles were nothing less than urban warfare on American streets.

The widespread nature of the rioting also demonstrated the demand for change and widespread unwillingness to continue to accept the racist status quo. The appearance of Dr. Martin Luther King in Los Angeles during the waning days of the 1965 rioting illustrates the growing community frustration. King was treated rudely by authorities after his arrival. During a private meeting with Mayor Sam Yorty and Police Chief William Parker, Yorty advised King that he "shouldn't have come here" (Stahl n.d.). Parker responded to King's presence with a table-pounding defense of his police department.

King was quickly dismissed by city authorities, and he was not treated much better when he went to the riot scene. His arrival with a ten-car motorcade was greeted with contempt by some of the residents who thought he was "grandstanding" (Stahl n.d.). His attempts to address the crowd were booed, and some began to throw litter at him.

A conversation with one of the young men in the crowd captured the gap between King and the rioters. At the young man's statement, "We won," King strongly reacted.

"How have you won?" King asked. "Homes have been destroyed, Negroes are lying dead in the streets, the stores from which you buy food and clothes are destroyed, and people are bringing you relief."

The youth answered, "We won because we made the whole world pay attention to us. The police chief never came here before; the mayor always stayed uptown. We made them come" (Stahl n.d.).

King's ineffectiveness with the Los Angeles rioters was echoed in the attempts of Newark's community leaders to curtail rioting. Even as Curvin was imploring the crowd to disperse, rocks and bottles began to fly.

The hostility of the Los Angeles and Newark white political leaders toward their black communities was remarkable, even in the context of that era's racial attitudes. In Los Angeles, the mayor quickly described the riots as the work of communist agitators. Yorty was an unabashed supporter of the police department and was later accused of running the "most racist campaign in the history of California" when he ran for mayor against Tom Bradley in 1969 (Simon 1988).

Yorty's comments were bland compared with the statements of the governor of New Jersey, Richard Hughes. In a press conference, Hughes described the Newark rioting as a "criminal insurrection." He stated, "This is a criminal insurrection by people who say they hate the white man but who really hate America." He was joined in the press conference by Mayor Addonizio, who also described the violence as the result of "an organization of people who hate America." Hughes was particularly blunt when addressing the murder of a fire department captain during the riot. "The people of Newark have to choose sides. They are either citizens of America or criminals who would shoot down a fire captain in the back and then depend on people to speak in platitudes about police brutality" (Bigart 1967).

These 1960s riots highlighted a lack of planning and coordination among government authorities. The after-action report by the Governor's Commission on the Los Angeles Riots detailed poor communication and confusion over responsibilities regarding the call-up and deployment of the National Guard. Per the commission's report, this leadership vacuum meant a crucial delay in deployment, which allowed the rioting to intensify.

The authorities in Newark also struggled. The Police Department appeared unprepared to deal with crowd disorder. A note from the log book of the New Jersey State Police during the riot paints a picture of a police department lacking direction. The entry noted, "There is still no organization within the Newark Police Department. The Fourth Precinct appears to be running its own show. There are no barricades. No requests for State Police from Director Spina" (Stahl n.d.).

The New Jersey National Guard appeared no better prepared. The guard unit deployed was all white, and after the riot, some black residents accused them of shooting out the windows of black-owned businesses and participating in beatings of arrested rioters. In a 2012 interview, Craig Mierop, a guardsman among those deployed to Newark during the riots, recalls the deployment aggravated the situation. He noted, "We added to the chaos on such a level that it just became crazy. When the riot came, we were totally unprepared and untrained" (St. Martin 2012).

Despite the widespread rioting—perhaps somewhat in response to it—the 1960s ushered in significant changes in the legal landscape for African Americans. The comprehensive Civil Rights Act of 1964 barred discrimination based on race across a broad spectrum of life, including public accommodation, employment, and education. The Voting Rights Act of 1965 also had a major impact. Michelle Alexander, author of *The New Jim Crow*, notes that the voting rates among black citizens in Southern states doubled and tripled. "Suddenly black children could shop in department stores, eat at a restaurant, drink from water fountains and go to amusement parks that were once off limits" (Alexander 2010, p. 38).

In the aftermath of rioting in the 1960s, President Lyndon B. Johnson created a commission charged with investigating the riots. The National Advisory Commission on Civil Disorders became known as the Kerner Commission for the appointed chair, former governor of Illinois Otto Kerner.[1] Its charge was to research the causes of the rioting and suggest steps to prevent future disorders. The commission found "White racism is essentially responsible for the explosive mixture which has been accumulating in our cities since the end of World War II" (National Advisory Commission on Civil Disorder 1969, p. 9). Among the ingredients in the "explosive mixture" the commission listed:

- "Pervasive discrimination and segregation in employment, education and housing, which have resulted in the continuing exclusion of great numbers of Negroes from the benefits of economic progress."
- "Black in-migration and white exodus, which have produced the massive and growing concentrations of impoverished Negroes in our major cities, creating a growing crisis of deteriorating facilities and services and unmet human needs."
- "The black ghettos where segregation and poverty converge on the young to destroy opportunity and enforce failure. Crime, drug addiction, dependency on welfare, and bitterness and resentment against society in general and white society in particular are the result." (National Advisory Commission on Civil Disorder 1969, p. 9)

The Kerner Commission famously predicted that without significant change, "Our nation is moving toward two societies, one black,
one white—separate and unequal" (National Advisory Commission
on Civil Disorder 1969, p. 1).

Along with the Civil Rights Act and Voting Rights Act, the
Johnson administration implemented a wide variety of programs
designed to reduce poverty. While the success of these Great Society
programs continues to be debated, there is little doubt that some of
them improved the economic circumstances for many African
Americans. The programs provided a significant safety net for many
of those in the lowest economic rungs in the country.

With these social changes and the removal of the legal vestiges of
racism and Jim Crow, policing, particularly police use of force,
became the central issue that continues to plague US race relations.

Since the 1960s, racial disturbances have even more clearly been
the result of a hostile relationship between the police and the black
community. This hostility provides ready fuel for an explosion when
a police force incident provides the spark.

Miami, Florida, was the site of the first major civil disturbance after
the 1960s. The riot had its origin in a vehicle pursuit by Miami Police in
December 1979. Police were pursuing a motorcycle driven by an
African American man, Arthur McDuffie. Initial reports said McDuffie
was killed when he wrecked his motorcycle during the pursuit. A later
coroner's report concluded that McDuffie's injuries were not consistent
with a motorcycle crash. This evidence was followed by the statement
of one of the responding officers that there was no crash, that McDuffie
had been beaten to death by officers using their flashlights.

Four officers were arrested and put on trial. On May 17, 1980, an
all-white jury found the officers not guilty, leading to three days of
rioting. Eighteen people were killed in the rioting, which was only
controlled after deployment of the Florida National Guard.

The sequence of a questionable police force incident, demands for
criminal charges, exoneration of the police officers, followed by rioting
in protest has become a template for post-1960s riots. The first city to
follow Miami through this deadly process was Los Angeles in 1992.

The 1992 riot in Los Angeles was the first US race riot in which
video documentation of the police action was shown across the nation.
The televised beating of Rodney King by white LAPD officers, the
subsequent trial, the not-guilty verdict for the officers, the rioting that
then ensued, the federal trial and guilty verdict for two of the officers,
and the criminal trials of riot participants whose assaults on people

were also captured on video make up the multi-year chapter of one of the ugliest race-related events in the history of this country. From the original traffic stop to the violent riots that exploded a year later, the episode provides graphic lessons on police tactics and force as well as riot preparation and planning by government bodies. The 1992 riot also provided a case study in the economic and social wreckage as a result of the rioting. The enormous damage caused by the rioting provides strong incentive for communities to work diligently on prevention, and effective response, should preventive efforts fall short.

Los Angeles, 1991: The Incident

On March 3, 1991, an African American man, Rodney King, was drunk and driving recklessly in San Fernando, near the northern edge of Los Angeles. When an officer attempted a traffic stop, King sped off, and one of the most significant events in US race relations was under way.

The pursuit began at around 12:45 a.m. when a California Highway Patrol (CHP) car tried to stop King for speeding. King was on parole and believed a DUI charge would send him back to prison. Despite pleas from his two passengers, King refused to stop, fleeing the police at speeds that at times exceeded 100 miles per hour. After a pursuit that lasted about fifteen minutes, King finally pulled over on Foot Hills Boulevard in the middle-class neighborhood of Lake View Terrace. Almost immediately, an estimated six patrol cars and fifteen additional police officers arrived on the scene. Among the police quickly on the scene were LAPD Sergeant Stacey Koon and officers Theodore Briseno, Timothy Wind, and Laurence Powell. A police helicopter that had followed the pursuit was overhead.

The CHP officers who had initiated the pursuit were a married couple, Tim and Melanie Singer. Tim Singer ordered King and his passengers to exit the car and lie prone on the ground. The passengers complied, but King ignored Singer's command. While Tim Singer moved to secure the passengers, Melanie Singer again ordered King out of the car. After a brief hesitation, King complied, but his behavior quickly raised the tension level. Melanie Singer testified King was smiling and waving at the helicopter. She ordered King to the ground and in response, he grabbed his right buttock, turned away from Singer, and shook his rear end at her. He then slowly complied with the order to get to the ground, and Singer, gun in hand, moved toward King to handcuff him.

Koon intervened, yelling at Singer, "Stand back. Stand back, we'll handle this" (Linder 2001, p. 2). Koon later testified he intervened because he believed Singer's approach, gun in hand, was a "lousy tactic."[2]

With King on the ground, Koon ordered Officers Powell, Wind, and Briseno to control him using a "swarm" technique. The "swarm" is simply multiple officers using body weight to control and handcuff a suspect (Linder 2001).

One officer grabbed King's legs, and the others attempted to control his arms. In a quick motion, King threw the officers off his back and got to his feet. Koon ordered the officers to back away and fired his taser at King, striking him in the back. King went to his knees groaning, but regained his feet and turned toward Koon. Koon fired the taser again, this time striking King in the chest. King again went down, but quickly got back on his feet and charged toward Powell.[3]

Across the street, awakened by the sirens and helicopter hovering overhead, George Holliday, manager in a plumbing company, went out on his apartment balcony to see what was happening. Holliday had just purchased a video recorder and decided to film the incident. The moment King charges toward Powell is the moment the Holliday tape begins.

Holliday's video of the beating was burned into the consciousness of America in the days and weeks that followed. Ed Turner, a vice president at CNN, noted that "Television used the tape like wallpaper" (Cannon 1999, p. 21). However, the video shown repeatedly after the event was different in a significant way from Holliday's original. Seconds after he began filming, Holliday moved the camera for a better view, causing a ten-second blur in the film. Holliday provided the entire tape to Los Angeles television station KTLA. The editors there decided to remove the blurred segment and also took out the initial three seconds, which showed King's charge toward Powell. This edited version of the tape was passed along by KTLA to national news outlets, including the major networks and CNN. This edited version was the one shown repeatedly across the country. Nearly a year after the event, CNN executives ordered the entire tape be used in future showings, but by that time, the perception of officers beating King without the least provocation had been well established.

The tape documents that the officers on the scene struck King with batons fifty-six times. The tape horrified most Americans, including some members of the LAPD. Paul Jefferson, an LAPD captain, recalled seeing the video (the unedited version) for the first time in the company of other officers in the Van Nuys police station. "It was unreal," he said. "When the officers saw the tape, there wasn't a word said. They just turned around and walked out with their heads down. Nobody said a word. They were in shock" (Cannon 1999, p. 24).

The chief of the LAPD, Darryl Gates, reacted strongly. Gates was a true believer in his police force, rarely missing a chance to proclaim it the finest department in the world. The tape made Gates "sick to my stomach." In writing about the incident later, he said, "To see my officers engaged in what appeared to be excessive use of force, possibly criminally excessive, to see them beat a man with their batons *fifty-six* times, to see a sergeant on the scene who did nothing to seize control, is something I never dreamed I would witness" (Cannon 1999, p. 24).

To the overwhelming majority of the country, black and white, the King beating looked like a clear-cut case of police brutality. A California poll taken shortly after the Holliday video was widely shown found that over 90% of those surveyed believed the police were guilty of excessive force (Linder 2001, p. 2). City authorities from Chief Gates to Mayor Tom Bradley, a former LAPD officer, quickly distanced themselves from the involved officers. Gates described the police behavior on the video as an "aberration" (Cannon 1999, p. 24).

Perhaps because the wider community viewed the scene with the same horror as the black community, there was no violence in the immediate aftermath of the incident. Over a year later, when an all-white jury found the officers not guilty, one of the worst race riots in the history of the country ensued. The riots exposed the racial divide in the country, and the televised beatings of Reginald Denny and others the first day of the rioting further widened the rift between black and white America.

Los Angeles, 1992: The King Verdict and Riot

Over a year after the incident, on April 29, 1992, the jury, in what was popularly referred to as the Rodney King case, sent word to the judge they had reached a verdict. Sergeant Koon and Officers Briseno, Wind, and Powell had been charged with a variety of crimes, including assault with a deadly weapon, assault under color of authority, and filing false reports. Koon had not struck King but was the supervisor on the scene, and he was charged as an accessory. LAPD was given two hours' notice, and the "not guilty" verdicts on all charges were broadcast at 3:15 p.m.

The trial had been moved out of Los Angeles at the request of the defense attorneys, who had argued that given the massive coverage of the King beating, a fair trial in the city was impossible. The judge agreed and moved the trial to Simi Valley, a largely white community outside of Los Angeles. With only a small number of African Americans in the jury pool and the use of peremptory challenges to exclude potential black jurors, an all-white jury was seated to hear the case.

The verdicts were a shock and surprise to the general public and the LA authorities. President George Bush spoke for most of the country when he said the verdict "stunned" him. Within the hour, Bush ordered the Justice Department to begin investigating potential federal charges against the officers (Cannon 1999, p. 374).

The reaction in South Central Los Angeles was less muted. Shortly after the verdict was broadcast, five men entered the Korean-owned Mr. Lee's liquor store in South Central LA. Antagonism between residents and the numerous Korean-owned markets in South Central was long-standing. The men each grabbed an armful of beer bottles and began to leave the store. David Lee, the shopkeeper, attempted to stop them. Lee was hit in the head, one of the men shouted, "This is for Rodney King!" and rioting was under way.

David Lee activated a robbery alarm and an LAPD police unit arrived and took a report. As the officers completed their report, they walked outside to find an angry and growing crowd. Patrol cars in the area were being besieged by roving bands throwing rocks and bottles. An "officer needs assistance" call at the intersection of Florence and Normandie, location of the liquor store, was put out at 5:43 p.m. Lieutenant Mike Moulin, the ranking officer, arrived at the scene to witness utter chaos, describing the intersection as uncontrollable. "The officers were being subjected to bricks, to huge pieces of concrete, to boards, to flying objects" (Cannon 1999, p. 287). Moulin ordered all officers out of the area. A reporter witnessing the police withdrawal described the crowd as empowered by the sight of the retreating patrol cars. "It was clearly a victory for them" (Cannon 1999, p. 288).

The situation went from bad to worse. When the police abandoned the area, they did nothing to stop traffic from entering, and the crowd became a mob that began to assault and rob drivers caught in the area. Whites, Latinos, and Asians were pulled from their cars and beaten. Television helicopters, hovering overhead, broadcast the attacks across the country as they were occurring. The lack of police response as well as the ferocity of the attacks was etched into the public consciousness in much the same manner as the King beating a year earlier.

At about 6:45 p.m., truck driver Reginald Denny entered the intersection near the liquor store. Denny, who had been listening to country music on his radio, was unaware of the violence in front of him. As he attempted to make his way through the crowds and destroyed cars in the intersection, rocks flew through his windows in the beginning of a broadcast episode of brutality that shocked the nation. Denny was dragged from his truck and hit with a claw hammer. Then a man named Damian Williams, standing right over Denny, hurled a hunk of concrete at Denny's head. Williams turned to the TV helicopter, pointed down at the bleeding body of Denny, and did a brief dance. Williams' assault and his "victory dance" became the primary image of the rioting.

While the scenes of the assaults on Denny and other victims in the area horrified the country, the absence of the police, as made clear by the broadcasts, facilitated the spread of disorder. Ted Koppel, anchor of the *Nightline* news show, commenting on the televised beating of Denny, noted, "live TV also becomes the carrier of a virus. At one and the same time, television conveys the fever of street violence and the impotence of the police. The beatings, the looting, the arson spread" (Cannon 1999, p. 307).

While the police withdrawal certainly was a key factor in the escalating violence, it was only the most apparent of a series of misjudgments that allowed the rioting to grow and endure.

Five days later, with the rioting largely burned out, Mayor Bradley lifted the dawn-to-dusk curfew and officially ended the riots. Fifty-four people lost their lives in the rioting, the highest death toll for any civil disorder in the country since the New York City draft riot in 1863. More than 2,300 people were injured in the rioting, and property losses exceeded $900 million, the highest total for any US riot. The number of buildings burned was more than four times that of the Watts riot in 1965. Thousands of businesses were looted and hundreds of mom and pop stores in the city were gone, never to come back.

Cincinnati, 2001

When the radio transmission of a foot pursuit in the Over-the-Rhine section of Cincinnati was broadcast at 2:15 a.m. on April 9, 2001, Cincinnati Police Officer Steven Roach joined the pursuit.[4] Roach, an experienced officer familiar with the warren of streets and alleys intersecting the neighborhood, believed he knew which way the man would run. Just a minute later, the suspect, a twenty-two-year-old black man named Timothy Thomas, rounded the corner into an alley just as Roach was approaching from the other direction, running, gun in hand.

There are two versions of what occurred in the seconds that followed. Roach later testified that Thomas reached for the waistline of his baggy pants, leading Roach to believe he was going for a gun. The second version, that the shooting was an unintentional discharge, was bolstered by Roach's immediate comment to a responding command officer in the seconds after the shooting, "Oh my god, it just went off" (Bronson 2006, p. 46).

The facts of the shooting quickly became irrelevant in the heightened racial tension of an unarmed black man shot by a white police officer. Some of the tension was related to a period of sustained media attention on use of force by Cincinnati police officers. The *Cincinnati Enquirer*, the city's major daily newspaper, had published a multiday special series focusing on excessive use of force by the city police. The logo that accompanied each story showed a black man, his face covered in blood. In addition, an often repeated story line was that of fifteen black men killed by police in the years since 1995. While the majority of these were clearly justified, in the view of many in the community, the fact that no white men had been killed in this period was considered evidence of racial bias by the Cincinnati police. Two days after the Thomas shooting, tension exploded into rioting at a City Council meeting.

What was scheduled as the weekly Law and Public Safety Committee meeting was overwhelmed by protesters demanding answers to the Thomas shooting. In retrospect, canceling the meeting would have been the prudent course, but council members elected to hold the meeting and ordered that no uniformed police officers were to attend. Uniformed police had become a regular presence at the meeting over the previous year due to the occasionally threatening behavior of a group of protesters in attendance at nearly every meeting.

While council members attempted to control the meeting, protesters climbed on tables and then locked the doors of council chambers, not allowing the political leaders to leave "until we get answers" (Bronson 2006, p. 57). The crowd only quieted when local attorney Ken Lawson, or "Law Dog" as he was known, began to speak about "all the brothers who have been choked and shot to death by the police" (Bronson 2006, p. 28).

After nearly three hours, the crowd left City Hall, breaking windows and ransacking offices as they left. They headed to confront the police, the crowd swelling as it moved the four blocks to the police headquarters building.

About two dozen officers were fanned out along the sidewalk in front of the headquarters, confronting a crowd that now numbered in the hundreds. In charge of the cops was Assistant Chief Ron Twitty. As the crowd pressed in on the officers, Twitty stepped to the front with a bullhorn. Believing it might soothe the crowd, he offered the bullhorn to one of the protest leaders. Instead of asking for calm, the man launched a profanity-laden attack on the cops. After breaking the windows at police headquarters and tearing down the US flag at a Police memorial site across the street, the crowd surged east into the Over-the-Rhine neighborhood, and rioting began.

Rioting continued for two days, and the disorder was only controlled with imposition of a curfew and deployment of state police at the request of the mayor. In the first day of the rioting, white drivers in Over-the Rhine were pulled from their cars and attacked. Yet there were no deaths reported as a result of the riot and the police, although fired on, did not fire a single round in return. One officer was hit in the stomach with a bullet, but his belt buckle deflected the round.

Property damage was extensive, estimated at $3.6 million (Rucker and Upton 2006, p. 10). Following the riots, a boycott of the city by black activists cost Cincinnati an estimated $10 million in convention and tourism revenue as Bill Cosby, Wynton Marsalis, Smokey Robinson, and other entertainers cancelled their Cincinnati appearances (Rucker and Upton 2006, p. 10). The more serious damage occurred in the years following the riots as crime surged and homicides escalated. Cincinnati, which had a well-deserved reputation as a safe city, saw homicides jump from a total of thirty-five in 2000 to seventy-six by 2003.

After the riots, the city, the Fraternal Order of Police, the Black United Front, and the American Civil Liberties Union entered mediated negotiations, resulting in what came to be known as the Collaborative Agreement. The agreement called for a number of changes to police procedure, and implementation of those changes was overseen by a monitoring team of experts from around the country. The central theme of the Collaborative Agreement was a focus on community policing and problem solving. Although resisted by police leadership early on, with time the agreement has come to be seen as the cornerstone of much-improved police–community relations.

Oakland, January 2009

The Bay Area Rapid Transit Police, or BART police as they are known locally, responded to a report of a large fight on a BART train in the early hours of New Year's Day. Oscar Grant, age twenty-four, was taken off the train by BART officers at the Fruitvale Station. Grant was detained on the train platform along with some other men. Multiple bystanders began filming the incident using their cellphones. The videos depict three officers, including Johannes Mehserle, who appear to be attempting to handcuff Grant, placing him face down on the platform. The officers struggled with Grant, trying to pull his arms behind his back. Unsuccessful in securing Grant's hands, Mehserle stands, pulls his service weapon, and fires a shot into Grant's back.

Witnesses, including Grant's friends, agreed that Mehserle announced, prior to the shooting, "Get back. I'm going to Tase him" (Maher 2011). Grant was taken to the hospital, where he died the next morning.

Video of the shooting was provided to local media outlets and posted to a number of websites. Over the following days, it was viewed millions of times around the world.

On the afternoon of January 9, a protest march on the Grant shooting turned violent as crowds set fires and broke windows. The police responded quickly and made a number of arrests. The crowd dispersed, leaving only property damage in its wake.

The pattern of protests devolving into riots continued as the Grant shooting moved through the legal process. Mehserle and his attorney claimed the shooting was accidental, a result of "weapons confusion."[5] Mehserle believed he had drawn his Taser rather than his service weapon. His version was supported by the eyewitness testimony, including from friends of Grant's who had been detained alongside him. Witnesses also describe Mehserle as shocked after he fired the shot, exclaiming "Shit. I shot him" (Bulwa 2011a).

Protests and rioting followed Mehserle's case through the criminal justice process. A year after the shooting, the Almeda County prosecutor filed a murder charge against Mehserle. Bail was set at $3 million. After a series of hearings, the trial began in October 2010.

In closing arguments, Mehserle's attorney reiterated the claim that the shooting was clearly accidental and urged the jury not to make "some sort of commentary on the state of relations between the police and the community in this country" (Bulwa 2011b, p. C1).

The judge ruled out a murder charge, noting the prosecution had not provided proof of premeditation on Mehserle's part. The jury was offered four potential outcomes, including acquittal. They found him guilty of the least serious offense, involuntary manslaughter. Mehserle was subsequently sentenced to four years in prison.

Ferguson, 2014

Ferguson, Missouri, seemed an unlikely place for race riots. Riots had typically occurred in bigger cities, whereas Ferguson, one of eighty-nine municipalities in St. Louis County, listed its population in the 2010 census as 21,000 people. About 67 percent of Ferguson residents were African American, and about 25 percent lived below the federal poverty level (Department of Justice, Civil Rights Division 2015, p. 6). On August 9, 2014, Ferguson joined the roster of US cities where police use of force and race intersected with violent results.

The time line on the shooting has been well documented by the Department of Justice report on the shooting death of Michael Brown. The following description of the events leading to the shooting, the shooting itself, and the immediate aftermath are taken from that report (Department of Justice 2015).

The incident began with Michael Brown and his friend Darien Johnson stealing some cigarillos from the Ferguson Market, a convenience store near the location of Brown's shooting. Video of that incident showed Brown taking some cigarillos from the clerk and shoving the clerk aside when he tried to stop Brown.[6] As Brown and Johnson left, the clerk called police, and a police broadcast was made with reference to "stealing" of cigarillos from the market. The broadcast included descriptions of Johnson and Brown.

Ferguson Police Officer Darren Wilson encountered Johnson and Brown walking down the middle of the street. Wilson stopped his car, and there was some conversation between him and the two men. Wilson said he simply asked the two to move to the sidewalk. Johnson said the officer told them to "get the fuck on the sidewalk" (Department of Justice 2015, p. 44). Brown and Johnson continued to walk in the street. Wilson turned his vehicle around, pulled past the two men, and then parked, blocking their way. He noted the cigarillos in Johnson's hand, and from the description previously broadcast, he realized he was confronting the two suspects in the Ferguson Market robbery. He radioed his location, asking for backup.

With Brown and Johnson standing nearly against the car door, Wilson attempted to exit the vehicle. Brown pushed the door back, not allowing Wilson to exit. Brown then reached into the car and began to swing at Wilson. Wilson pulled his gun, Brown attempted to take the gun from him, and a shot was fired, striking Brown in the hand. Brown stepped away from the car and began to run away. Wilson broadcast "shots fired," exited the car, and began to chase Brown. Brown stopped, turned, and faced the officer, then charged toward him. Wilson fired several shots at Brown, who fell dead only a few feet short of the officer.

Immediately after the shooting, the situation on the street grew tense. Crowds gathered as officers began to secure the crime scene. The crowd began to grow hostile with chants of "We need to kill these motherfuckers" coming from some in the crowd (Department of Justice 2015, p. 8).

Approximately twenty minutes after the shooting, the Ferguson police chief notified the St. Louis County Police Department (SLCPD) of the shooting and turned the investigation over to them. At the scene, Brown's body was covered with white sheets.

Much has been made of the fact that the crime scene took nearly four hours to process. This led to a widely reported complaint from Brown's family and others implying that authorities were negligent in taking an extended period of time to process the scene. "The delay helped fuel the outrage," said Patricia Bynes, a democratic party committee member in Ferguson. "It was very disrespectful to the community and the people who live there. It also sent the message from law enforcement that, 'We can do this to you any day, any time, in broad daylight, and there's nothing you can do about it'" (Bosman and Goldstein 2014). In fact, the delay was due partly to growing chaos at the scene that, in the view of the police, threatened the safety of the investigators. As the DOJ report notes, when the SLCPD received the request to process the scene, their crime scene investigators were involved in a hostage situation fifteen minutes away. On their way to the scene, automatic gunfire in the area was reported, threatening officers and civilians (Department of Justice 2015, p. 8). Brown's body was removed from the scene about four hours after the shooting.

Concern with the growing crowd had led the officers responsible for scene integrity to request additional officers for crowd control. Another contingent of officers was dispatched, along with police canines.[7] The crowd was also inflamed by the rumor that Brown had been shot while holding his hands in up in a surrender gesture. The origin of this "hands-up" narrative was Darrien Johnson, listed as Witness 101 in the DOJ report.

Immediately after the shooting, Johnson ran home and changed his shirt, afraid of being identified by the police. He then went to Brown's home and told them what had happened, including his story of Brown's hands-up gesture.

Johnson's story of Brown's "execution" while his hands were raised was reported and spread by the local and national media arriving on the scene. On its website, CNN identified Johnson as "an eyewitness" to the shooting as if he were a neutral observer.

There were two other reported incidents in those first hours that escalated the situation. Reportedly, a police canine officer had allowed his dog to urinate on a makeshift memorial for Brown. Furthermore, as the police left the scene, there was a claim that an officer had intentionally driven his car over the memorial, destroying it (Follman 2014). Whether rumor or fact, the stories contributed to the perception of a brutal police presence.

The narrative of a young, unarmed black man shot down by police quickly generated widespread media interest. The "hands-up!" characterization of the incident swiftly became a major theme. As media outlets descended on Ferguson the next day, protests over the shooting grew larger. A peaceful memorial march and candlelight vigil devolved into violence as crowds lit fires, threw rocks and bottles at the police, and looted businesses. In the days that followed, disorder continued, spreading from Ferguson to Clayton, the county seat. Protests on the police shooting in Ferguson were not limited to that area, with protest demonstrations occurring in more than 100 cities in the United States (Freelon 2014).

Over the next few days, protests on the shooting went international and included Tibetan monks marching in solidarity with Ferguson demonstrators (Varghese 2014). Even ISIS weighed in on the controversy, claiming their brand of Islamic fundamentalism was needed in Ferguson (Mekhennet 2014).

Confrontations with media generated much of the controversy over police response to the disorder. Local politicians joined the protesters and were arrested. Ferguson police officers in military garb were filmed arresting *Washington Post* reporters, an incident that drew disparaging comments from President Barack Obama. Videos posted on social media showed police officers pointing guns at protesters; one officer was recorded as saying "Get the fuck out of my face" (GlobalNewsCentre.com 2014). Another was recorded taunting protesters, yelling, "Bring it, you fucking animals, bring it!" (Terkel 2014).

On August 14, the governor of Missouri, Jay Nixon, announced that the State Highway Patrol was taking over responsibility for police operations in Ferguson. Nixon named Patrol Captain Ron Johnson as commander of the Ferguson operations. Johnson was an African American who had grown up in Ferguson, and his appointment was clearly intended to ease the racial tension. Nixon announced a curfew from midnight to 5 a.m. and added that the police would provide plenty of warning to protesters. He also promised not to use the military equipment and tactics that had been widely criticized in the previous days.

In spite of Nixon's good intentions and Johnson joining a protest march in the early evening, late that night, protests again morphed into looting and arson. As the violence intensified after midnight, the military tactics decried by Nixon, including use of armored personnel carriers and tear gas, were deployed against rioters. The next day, August 18, Nixon announced the National Guard was to be deployed to "help restore peace and order and to protect the citizens of Ferguson" (Hartmann 2014). He also announced that there would be no curfew on the night of August 18.

Protests and sporadic violence in Ferguson continued over the following months. Intense media coverage persisted, with police treatment of the media a continuing issue. The media in Ferguson included correspondents from around the world, and the prickly relationship with police reached absurd levels. Two German reporters claimed they were arrested by a Ferguson officer who would only identify himself as "Donald Duck" (The Local 2014).

On November 24, the grand jury hearing the Brown shooting case declined to indict Wilson. The finding was announced by County Prosecutor Robert McCullough in the early evening hours, and rioting broke out shortly after. The violence was described by St. Louis County Police Chief Jon Belmar as "probably worse than the worst night we had in August" (Alcindor et al. 2014). Belmar noted he had personally heard 150 gunshots. An estimated crowd of 300 rioters was eventually dispersed. One police officer was shot, two police cars were burned, and those area businesses that had not been attacked during August protests were burned and looted (Alcindor et al. 2014).

Baltimore, 2015

The in-custody death of Freddie Gray on April 19, 2015, became the most recent in a highly publicized string of African American men dying at the hands of police. A week earlier, at 8:42 a.m., Baltimore officer Lieutenant Brian Rice rode his police bike toward Freddie Gray. Gray turned, made eye contact with Rice, and then took off running.[8] Rice and two other bike officers pursued Gray, who surrendered after a short pursuit. Gray was placed on his stomach and handcuffed. A knife was found on him, and he was placed in a prisoner transport van.[9] In violation of department policy, the officers failed to secure Gray with a seatbelt.

In route, Gray was screaming in the back of the van and the driver, Officer Caesar Goodson, stopped to allow the arresting officers to check on him. The officers removed Gray from the van, applied flex-cuffs, and put shackles on his ankles. Gray was reloaded in the van lying face down on the floor. The van made two other stops. At one stop, Sergeant Alicia White opened the back door of the van, and per the prosecutor's report, tried to talk to Gray. Despite a lack of response from Gray, she took no action and the van continued to the police station.

On arrival, the officers called medics, who found Gray critically and severely injured and suffering cardiac arrest. Gray was taken to the hospital, where he was in a coma and then died a week later. The prosecutor's report states Gray's death was the "result of being hand-cuffed, shackled by his feet and unrestrained inside of the [Baltimore Police Department] wagon" (Peralta 2015).

Gray's arrest, captured on video, generated protests beginning on April 18. When he was pronounced dead on April 19, the protests grew. Six Baltimore officers involved in the incident were suspended. The Department of Justice announced it would initiate an investigation. In the face of growing protests, Maryland Governor Larry Hogan dispatched a contingent of state police to assist the Baltimore Police.

On April 25, peaceful protests began to turn violent. Rocks and bottles were thrown at the police and a 7-11 store was looted. Five Baltimore officers were injured. City officials described the disorder as "pockets of individuals causing disturbances" (Ortiz 2015).

The following day, Gray's funeral was held. That night, protests turned violent, including looting of stores across the city. The governor declared a state of emergency and ordered the National Guard into the city. The next day, Baltimore's mayor, Stephanie Rawlings-Blake, ordered a curfew from 10 p.m. to 5 a.m., which limited further violence. The Baltimore Police Department turned over the investigation of Gray's death to the state's attorney for Baltimore, Marilyn Mosby. Mosby is African American, and her husband was a Baltimore City Council member who represents the city district where Gray's death occurred.

On May 1, Mosby announced criminal charges against six Baltimore police officers, including Rice and White. Three of the officers are African American and the other three are white. Charges against the officers included second-degree murder, manslaughter, assault, and misconduct in office.

Discussion

The character of race riots has continued to evolve in the new century. The Los Angeles riot of 1992 was the last race riot with a significant number of deaths. The Cincinnati riots of 2001 did not result in a single death, and the police, although fired on, did not expend a single bullet in return. In the series of riots following the criminal prosecution process of BART Officer Mehersle in Oakland, no lives were lost, and in both Ferguson and Baltimore, despite repeated violent episodes, no deaths have occurred. This is indisputably progress of a dubious sort, given the pattern of increases in shootings and homicides in the periods after rioting. Those deaths are not perceived or recorded as riot-related but tend to be regarded as business as usual.

Although separated in time by nearly fifty years, some of the dynamics of race-related rioting remain consistent. Almost uniformly, the initial public response by officials was to deny and downplay the seriousness of the situation. Any preriot planning was apparently absent, and coordination among officials at the local, state, and federal levels typically came only after rioting was well under way. Despite clear lessons from earlier riots, police officials remained reluctant to act decisively in the early stages of disorder.

Police officials were largely inept in dealing with the media prior to disorder and in the midst of rioting. In Cincinnati, as racial tension built, police leaders chose silence even as the local media painted the department as rife with race-related brutality. The most outrageous claims made daily on talk radio and in public demonstrations were ignored, with the result that the public began to assume many of the accusations were factual. Then Cincinnati Police Chief Tom Streicher regrets not responding more forcefully. "One of our biggest mistakes was zero communication. That let the city start boiling" (Bronson 2006, p. 133).

Ferguson, a small city with part-time public officials and a small police department, found itself in the middle of a media tsunami. Every statement and action became the subject of intense scrutiny and second-guessing. Ridicule and critiques from "experts" flourished as Ferguson officials, totally unprepared and inexperienced in media relations, struggled to respond coherently to what became an international event.

Statements made and actions taken during the formative stages of rioting consisted largely of wishful thinking. In Newark in 1965, Mayor Hugh Addonizio took pains to describe the previous night's disorder as "not a race riot." In Cincinnati, the day after a disorderly crowd ransacked city offices and broke windows, city officials publically stated about a dozen windows were broken. Yet the contractor responsible for fixing the damage stated he replaced 200 windows (Bronson 2006, p. 35). In Baltimore, after the first night of violence, officials minimized it as "pockets of individuals causing disturbances" (Ortiz 2015).

The 1992 Los Angeles riot provides the clearest template for what not to do in the initial stages of disorder. The LAPD withdrawal from Florence and Normandie left a vacuum of lawlessness that was filled by violent assaults televised across the country. The lessons from Los Angeles were ignored in Cincinnati, when as protesters gathered at City Hall, officials ordered uniformed police out of the area, believing their presence would inflame the crowd. Instead, the lack of police presence animated the crowd, sending the message that riotous behavior would be tolerated. That mistake was amplified a short time later when the acting chief, confronting a disorderly crowd at police headquarters, handed protest leaders a bullhorn, believing that "letting them vent" would calm the crowd. In fact, faced with a line of police ordered not to take action, the crowd was emboldened to surge into the nearby Over-the-Rhine neighborhood, assaulting people and looting stores (Bronson 2006, p. 16).

The deluded belief that "everything will be all right" was best personified by LAPD Chief Daryl Gates in the hours following the King verdict. As the violence in South Central LA intensified, Gates chose to attend a fund-raising dinner in faraway Brentwood (Cannon 1999, p. 289). Gates was aware of the escalating violence before his departure when he heard a report from an intelligence officer that described the Florence and Normandie area as "out of control" and a second report of crowds gathering at the Foothills Police Station combined with phone threats of "We are going to start killing fucking cops!" (Cannon 1999, p. 289).

Statements by public officials in the early stages can act as catalysts for either encouraging or discouraging disorder. In some instances, officials jumped to deploring police action without the benefit of any investigative process. Just days after the Brown shooting, Missouri Governor Jay Nixon stated "a vigorous prosecution must now be pursued." Nixon added, "We have a responsibility to come together, and do everything we can to achieve justice for [Brown's] family" (FoxNews.om 2014).

Nixon also appeared reluctant to take decisive action to gain control in Feguson. The same day he dispatched National Guard troops, he ended the curfew.

In Los Angeles, Mayor Tom Bradley's televised comments following the King verdict led to criticism that he was inviting a riot. Clearly angry about the verdict, Bradley said the "senseless" verdict had left him "speechless." The mayor then attacked the jury. "Today, the jury told the world that what we all saw with our own eyes was not a crime. . . . We saw what we saw, and what we saw was a crime. No, we will not tolerate the savage beating of our citizens by a few renegade cops" (Cannon 1999, p. 289). Bradley went on to call for calm, a plea that fell flat after his denunciation of the verdict.

In Cincinnati, Mayor Charlie Luken went on CNN after the first night of rioting and said, "There is a great deal of frustration within the community, which is understandable. We've had way too many deaths in our community at the hands of the police" (Bronson 2006, p. 39). Luken's comments were widely seen as justifying the rioting and ignoring the fact that the Cincinnati Police use of deadly force was significantly lower than nearly every other major city in the country (Rahtz 2001, p. 1).

After the BART shooting in Oakland, Mayor Ron Dellums joined protesters in a march to City Hall. He took a bullhorn and told the crowd, "I sense your pain and your frustration." The crowd responded with anger and boos, forcing Dellums to retreat into his City Hall office. The crowd then began to burn and loot nearby businesses (McCarthy 2009).

Comments from political leaders have an impact on police behavior long after the rioting is over. In the years after the riots,

Cincinnati police engaged in a slowdown as officers withdrew from normal enforcement activities. Arrests declined, and violence spiked. The year after the riots, the city's homicide numbers broke a fifteen-year record. Improved medical emergency care for shooting victims likely kept the death toll from surging even higher. Shootings escalated from about 80 a year before the riot to more than 350 in 2005 (Bronson 2006, p. 146). A similar pattern of police withdrawal and increasing crime occurred in Los Angeles after the 1992 riots.

The impact of riots in a city echo long after the fires are put out. Many of the small businesses burned or looted can ill afford to reopen, leaving neighborhoods bereft of many retail services counted on by community residents. Perhaps most damaging is middle-class flight from the city, taking with them the tax base and glue for community cohesion.

Events in Ferguson and other widely reported force incidents have clearly exposed the racial rift that continues to challenge our country. When these incidents escalate into rioting, the schism widens, and the crucial relationship between police and their communities suffers damage that is difficult to overcome.

Notes

1. Kerner was later imprisoned on corruption charges related to a stock scandal.

2. Koon's intervention in the incident strikes many police officers as unusual. He was out of his jurisdiction and the traffic stop was initiated by the Highway Patrol. Koon's rationale for his intervention was his belief that Melanie Singer, the CHP officer involved, was endangering herself through poor tactics.

3. The taser used by Koon against King had nowhere near the effectiveness of the taser currently in use by police.

4. At the time of the riot in Cincinnati described in this section, the author was a lieutenant with the Cincinnati Police Department assigned to the Police Academy.

5. In April 2015, a seventy-three-year-old part-time reserve officer in Tulsa fatally shot a suspect in an eerily similar "weapons confusion" incident. Almost immediately, that officer was charged with manslaughter.

6. Brown's push of the clerk made what would have been a misdemeanor theft into a robbery, a felony. The worth of the cigarillos is immaterial.

7. Many departments prohibit the use of police dogs in crowd control. Their use invokes images of dogs turned loose on civil rights marchers in the

1960s, and such use would certainly inflame racial tension. Turning a dog loose in a crowd situation would be a highly questionable use of force.

8. In *Illinois v. Wardlow* (528 US 119; 2000), the Supreme Court ruled that unprovoked fleeing from the police created reasonable suspicion and justified an investigative stop of the individual.

9. Gray was charged with carrying a switchblade knife. However, state attorney Marilyn Mosby said the knife, based on the size of its blade, was not illegal. That led to the charge of unlawful arrest against the officers.

4

Learning from History

We recommend that the police and militia work out, at the earliest possible date, a detailed plan for joint action in the control of race riots.
— Report of the 1919 Chicago Commission on Riots

It was the first call after the verdicts. . . . We were the friendly neighborhood cops one minute, the next minute we were lunch meat.

— LAPD Sergeant Don Schwartzer (1992)

The challenge for public officials is two-fold. First is to create a partnership between community members and the police that effectively controls crime and disorder in the context of a compassionate and respectful relationship. This relationship builds trust in the community that the police are truly there to protect and serve, and when incidents occur that strain that relationship, there is an open and transparent strategy to address it. Effectively establishing such a relationship helps immunize the community against riots.

Because police use of force is likely to be a major factor creating tension in the relationship, a key ingredient has to be a significant effort reviewing standards and training for use of force and a review of the investigative and legal process following force incidents. The goal is community consensus on a process that is both transparent and mindful of the integrity of the investigation.

47

The second challenge is a planning process that outlines police and government response if and when riots occur. Although police action may be the spark for community disorder, a host of social and economic factors make up the kindling. A process addressing not only police action but other factors underlying community tension can be addressed as well.

From the police perspective, strategies to effectively manage legal protests should be developed jointly with community members. Tactics to quickly and humanely suppress disorder, should it occur, have to be a primary focus of these discussions. Each situation brings its own set of challenges, and history can provide a starting point for these difficult conversations. A short review of previous riots and subsequent government responses, good and bad, will eliminate some preventable mistakes.

This process should generate significant buy-in from community members as well as detailed agreements among state, local, and federal authorities. These agreements should cover the circumstances for deployment of state and federal resources; the timeline for deployment of these resources; agreements on command, control, and coordination; and shared cost considerations. The planning should cover steps to help with community recovery should disorder occur.

Every community brings a unique set of circumstances to the planning effort, but there are some steps that should generate wide agreement. There are also some hard lessons from past race riots providing important guideposts in the planning effort. Preventing and responding effectively to riots requires seeking consensus in development of short- and long-term strategy. Lessons from history providing a starting point for these discussions follow.

Diversity

Police critics and police leaders are generally in agreement that the police force should ideally mirror the community they are policing. For police agencies, diversity is a business necessity. A heavily white law enforcement agency policing a majority African American community faces a significant burden where even the most routine police action is likely to be perceived as racially influenced.

It is no accident that in early race riots (Washington in 1919, Los Angeles in 1943), white members of a segregated military were the primary aggressors. President Harry S Truman desegregated the military in 1948, but US police departments have been slow to follow. African American communities were policed by overwhelmingly white police departments well into the 1960s. It was only the passage of the Civil Rights Act and the unrelenting efforts of the NAACP and other groups that began to change the complexion of American policing. Although a diverse police force is no guarantee of police–community harmony, the very presence of a diverse group of officers carries a degree of legitimacy that would be difficult if not impossible to achieve by a largely white police organization.

When officials in New York City deputized 300 African American women to assist in controlling the Harlem riot in 1943, it was in recognition that these women carried a legitimacy in the community that the white police force did not. The same dynamic was evident in Ferguson in 2014 when Missouri Governor Jay Nixon appointed Captain Ron Johnson, an African American, to lead the effort to end the rioting in that city. Nixon's action was clearly rooted in the belief that the Ferguson Police Department leadership was not respected or trusted by the black community.

Despite significant gains in police employment by African Americans since the 1960s, policing remains a primarily white occupation, even in communities where African Americans are in the majority. The racial gap is smaller in large cities, many of which operate under court consent decrees dating to the 1970s, which mandated hiring a certain percentage of minorities and women.

A study reviewing the minority composition of a community compared with the minority representation in the police department provides a picture of how large the gap remains. The survey, published by the US Bureau of Justice Statistics, found, "In hundreds of police departments across the country, the percentage of whites on the force is more than 30 percentage points higher than in the communities they serve" (Ashkenas and Park 2014). The biggest gaps tended to reside not in large cities but in suburban areas, where the black population has increased significantly over the past several years. Ferguson is a good example of this phenomenon. Ferguson had a black population 55 percentage points higher than the percentage of African Americans on its police force (Ashkenas and Park 2014). Similar findings exist in communities across the country.

Noting the importance of diversity and its relative absence in police organizations is the easy part. Describing effective solutions is more difficult. Police departments typically operate under restrictive civil service rules mandating a hiring process that relies heavily on written test instruments. The education gap between whites and blacks is well documented, so it is hardly a surprise that whites as a group score higher on these tests than do black candidates. The consent decrees in many cities dictate the creation of separate civil service eligibility lists for blacks and whites, thus mitigating the scoring difference. This process is sometimes derided in the community and within police departments as contributing to the hiring of less qualified individuals.[1]

Cedric Alexander is a forty-year police veteran and head of the National Organization of Black Law Enforcement Executives. He believes that recruiting African Americans as police officers is more difficult today than it was early in his career. Two factors that he and other recruiters mention are increased opportunity in other career fields and antipolice feelings among young African Americans. Kevin Minor, a recruiting officer for the St. Louis County Police, sees the strongest anticop sentiments in group settings. Minor, who was on duty during Ferguson protests and called an "Uncle Tom" by crowd members, tries to speak to potential recruits on an individual basis, but he worries that black candidates will be turned off to policing by Ferguson-type events.

Some prospective candidates see the situation in places like Ferguson as a challenge. Benny Newsom, an African American and a criminal justice major in St. Louis, had a different reaction. "I think that it kind of enhanced my urge to actually go further in law enforcement," he said (Kaste 2014). Newsom told an interviewer he "wants to be part of a new generation of American police—a generation that's more community-oriented and less prone to using force" (Kaste 2014).

The recruitment of minority candidates has become a significant element in the human resources effort of many police departments. Police cadet programs focusing on minority youth, mentoring programs in inner-city schools, and summer camp programs are just a few of the efforts currently used to increase minority hiring. Recruiting is an area where some creativity could provide significant results and where a cooperative effort between the police department and community could help build a more healthy relationship.

Although diversity is a key ingredient in the police–community relationship, diversity alone is no panacea. In Baltimore, a city with an African American mayor, an African American police commissioner, and a police department where nearly 50 percent of the officers are African American, racial tensions remain (West 2015). The lesson for police leaders is diversity is only the first of many challenges.

Transparency

Transparency is word thrown around discussions of police reform nearly as often as *diversity*. Transparency, like diversity, is a business essential for effective police operations. Transparency becomes most critical in the aftermath of a serious police use of force incident. In light of the current distrust of the police by many in the African American community, incidents involving white police officers and black citizens are viewed through the lens of racial suspicion. There is little faith in internal police review of these incidents, and that mistrust extends to prosecutors who decide whether to pursue criminal charges against the officer(s) involved. This mistrust of local prosecutors is most glaring in the repeated calls for federal intervention and investigation of police force incidents.

Police leaders have a history of resisting calls for independent oversight bodies. J. Edgar Hoover, the first director of the FBI, reacted to early calls for citizen review by claiming it would "paralyze the police" (Rahtz 2003). Yet even prior to 2000, a majority of large city departments had some mechanism for external citizen review (Purnick 1996). The issue is one of trust, and the challenge is designing a system that ensures investigative integrity and transparency. Civilian oversight groups reviewing police force incidents are now a feature of many police jurisdictions. In some cases, these oversight bodies provide independent investigations, totally outside of the police department. In others, they operate in a fashion similar to an outside auditor, reviewing and critiquing the police investigations.[2]

Outside investigations of police misconduct are not a cure-all for police–community relations. The expectation that such outside review will yield vastly different results compared with traditional internal investigations is not supported by the facts (Rahtz 2003). In a study comparing findings of police internal investigations with those of external bodies, Perez and Muir (2005) found "the internal system was more prone to find misconduct."

However, judging these efforts simply on the basis of outcomes is short-sighted. The issue is less one of outcomes than of establishing a system that gains the trust of the community. The bottom-line case for independent review is simple and should resonate with police officers.

> Ask any cop if he believes the Internal Revenue Service, the Environmental Protection Agency, or any other governmental group

should be subject to ongoing monitoring and review by external bodies. The overwhelming majority of officers, like other informed citizens, recognize the importance of outside review to ensure agency integrity and compliance with the rules. Yet many of the same officers who would scoff at the idea of the IRS or any other government entity policing itself strongly oppose any sort of civilian oversight. Police power and authority are unmatched by any other governmental entity. This fact argues for more oversight, not less. (Rahtz 2003)

The case for transparency goes beyond investigation of force incidents. Recruiting, training, budget, use of force policy, disciplinary procedures, and the citizen complaint process are all areas where increased transparency could have a major impact on improving community legitimacy.

Investing in Legitimacy

The relationship between the community and its police force must be the single highest priority for police leadership. Like any relationship, hard work and effective communications are key elements. In the past, notions like police legitimacy were the focus of a public information officer who acted as a media liaison. The appointment of community liaison officers to attend neighborhood meetings was another frequently used option.

A variety of programs have become popular. These efforts include open houses at police stations, shop-with-a-cop programs involving officers acting in a Santa Claus–type role, and dozens of others. These programs take officers momentarily out of their law enforcement role and cast them as compassionate helpers of the community. These efforts typically generate positive media coverage for the department, which is often the goal of the program.

The programs all have some value but typically are utilized without a full appreciation for the larger context. Even as programs to improve community relations have grown, they continue to occupy a fringe area of the police mission.

That context is the understanding that *every* action taken by *every* officer reflects not only on the individual department but on policing as a whole. A highly publicized event like the riots in Ferguson creates fallout across the country, affecting police officers working in every jurisdiction. The legitimacy of a police department in its own community will be affected by these high-profile events. Serious police leaders recognize the potential damage to their departments and will quickly take steps to address it.

Though these larger events have an impact, day-to-day citizen interaction is where police legitimacy is reinforced or degraded. Every time an officer is rude, condescending, sarcastic, or inattentive, police legitimacy takes a hit. By contrast, an effective police professional will conduct him- or herself in such a manner that even the ugliest encounters will not degrade or dehumanize another.

Most officers understand that there is a personal investment in treating citizens with respect and dignity. A driver treated discourteously is a potential juror or a voter considering a tax levy to support the police department. The suspect who gets treated roughly during an arrest will statistically encounter other officers in the future. These officers may face an individual acting out of fear and rage, who suddenly turns a routine encounter violent.

Legitimacy can best be viewed as a bank account. All police departments have a certain trust balance in their account. Actions by every officer—from those answering the phone to those responding to a call—will add to or subtract from this account. When major incidents occur, the trust account needs to be at a level that will withstand the event fallout.

Particularly in high-profile events, with a department under the media microscope, racist, stupid, or simply unprofessional behavior takes on added importance. A review of the computer messages sent among LAPD officers after the Rodney King beating reinforced the public view that the officers' behavior was not a controlled use of force but rather punishment inflicted on King. Stacy Koon's notification of a "big time use of force" after the incident generated a reply from a dispatch supervisor of "I'm sure the lizard didn't deserve it. Ha, ha" (Cannon 1999, p. 38).

Lawrence Powell, one of the LAPD officers convicted in the King incident, exchanged messages with another officer that displayed at best a serious lack of professionalism. Almost immediately after the incident, Powell sent a message to Officer Corina Smith.

Powell: Oops.
Smith: Oops, what?
Powell: I haven't beaten anyone this bad in a long time. (Cannon 1999, p. 38)

Racist texts between officers were also discovered. After responding to a family trouble run involving African Americans, Powell texted another officer that the situation was out of the movie *Gorillas in the Mist*. That officer responded back, "Let me guess who be the parties" (Cannon 1999, p. 222).

Racist emails became part of the story in Ferguson. The Department of Justice Report on the Ferguson Police Department lists a number of racist emails originating from Ferguson city officials. Although none of the emails were linked to police officers, the overall impression is of a city administration that tolerates racist behavior. Some examples listed in the DOJ report were:

- A November 2008 email stated that President Barack Obama would not be president for very long because "what black man holds a steady job for four years?"
- A March 2010 email mocked African Americans through speech and familial stereotypes, using a story involving child support. One line read: "I be so glad that dis be my last child support payment! Month after month, year after year, all dose payments!"
- An April 2011 email depicted President Barack Obama as a chimpanzee.
- A May 2011 email joked: "An African-American woman in New Orleans was admitted into the hospital for a pregnancy termination. Two weeks later she received a check for $5,000. She phoned the hospital to ask who it was from. The hospital said, 'Crimestoppers.'" (Department of Justice 2015)

The existence of these emails reinforces the perception that not only the police but the entire city administration is racist. In this atmosphere, encounters between police officers and African American citizens, difficult under the best of circumstances, are complicated by the belief that race is a driving factor in the police behavior.

Behavior as described above delegitimates the police and inserts racial suspicion into the daily interaction between police and citizens. While police and political leaders will decry the lack of community involvement and the power of the "don't snitch" culture, they are less likely to recognize their own role in reinforcing a view of police as racist and uncaring intruders in the neighborhood.

The maintenance of community legitimacy is the context in which all police activity occurs. Strategies to heighten and strengthen that legitimacy will pay significant benefits, reduce crime, and lower the risk for community disorder (the issue of police legitimacy is dealt with in detail in Chapter 7).

Riot Tactics

A review of previous riots reveals clear lessons on planning and preparation. These lessons include direction on some issues and more general guidance on others. The major lesson is that lack of planning and leadership in the early stages of disorder is a recipe for disaster. The riots in Detroit in 1943, Newark in 1965, and Los Angeles in 1992 all were characterized by poor communication and leadership among local and state officials. More recent events confirm the persistence of these issues. James Knowles, the mayor of Ferguson, watched in frustration as rioters took over the city while officials at the local, county, and state level "sent opposing signals, changed course and, at times, failed to talk to one another"—what Knowles acknowledges "as a collective failure of leadership from his office on up" (Davey and Vega 2014).

As events unfolded in Baltimore in the spring of 2015, communication issues plagued the response to the rioting. While Larry Hogan, the governor of Maryland, quickly mobilized the National Guard and other resources, the legally required request from Baltimore officials did not come until after the first day's disorder. Hogan blamed the Baltimore mayor for the delay, stating in a press conference, "When the mayor called me, which quite frankly we were glad that she finally did, instantly we signed the executive order" (McCabe 2015). While Hogan has received praise for his immediate response, the absence of any predisorder planning among state and local officials was apparent.

The Baltimore communications snafu is hardly unique. The sometimes strained relationships among political and police leaders can impede effective response, allowing needless deaths and injuries, escalated economic damage, and a degraded relationship between the police and community. The 1992 Los Angeles riot is a prime example.

LAPD planning and preparation before the 1992 riot was hampered by false assumptions and poor preparation. The main riot response unit, the LAPD Metro Unit, had training and equipment to quickly suppress early rioting behavior. But as the LAPD after-action report noted, "Metropolitan Division pre-riot recommendations for deployment, tactics and training were ignored. A request to obtain, train with and deploy non-lethal weapons well in advance of the riots was ignored. Advice concerning the most effective way to pre-position the division was similarly ignored" (Cannon 1999, p. 274).

Furthermore, the LAPD brass believed if there was to be rioting, it would not occur until after dark, leaving time to deploy the necessary resources. When the head of the Metro Unit requested to be deployed during the day in anticipation of the King verdicts, he was told by a deputy chief, "Riots don't happen during the day" (Cannon 1999, p. 264).

The lack of planning started from the top of the LAPD with Chief Daryl Gates. He discouraged riot planning and ordered that no written record be made of meetings discussing potential rioting. Gates said, "I don't want to put the LAPD in the position of predicting a riot. I don't want us to be accused of issuing a self-fulfilling prophecy" (Cannon 1999, p. 264).

Gates was not alone in shunning riot preparation. LA Mayor Tom Bradley believed riot preparation could be a provocation. Even after the riots, Bradley and others who criticized the LAPD withdrawal "never acknowledged that their own attempts to restrain the police had contributed to inadequate deployment and preparation" (Cannon 1999, p. 271).

While the LAPD commanders received criticism for the police withdrawal in the early stages of the 1992 rioting, poor planning and decision making left the on-scene commanders without adequate resources to respond effectively. The biggest mistake was the assumption that guilty verdicts in the King case were a sure thing. "If we were not prepared for any one thing, we were not prepared for four not-guilty verdicts," said one LAPD commander after the riots (Cannon 1999, p. 264).

Above and beyond the lack of preparation, the clearest tactical lesson provided by riot review is that withdrawal of police in the early stages of disorder acts as a catalyst leading to serious riot conditions. The withdrawal of the LAPD in the beginning stages of the rioting in 1992 created a vacuum that escalated the mob violence that followed. The Christopher Commission Report noted the "failure to respond aggressively and in force appears to have been a significant tactical mistake" (Cannon 1999, p. 294).

Ten years later, Cincinnati's political and police leaders made the same mistake. The decision to order police officers out of the Public Safety Committee meeting and the later failure to disperse a disorderly crowd at police headquarters had results similar to the LAPD withdrawal a decade earlier.

A related lesson is that looting can and should be aggressively addressed. Although some looting activity may accompany the initial stages of disorder when police may find they are unable to respond quickly, the decision to stand aside and allow looting represents an abdication of responsibility and has long-term effects.

In riots through the 1960s, police shootings of looters accounted for a significant portion of the death toll of those events. In 1985, the Supreme Court decision *Tennessee v. Garner* (471 US 1, 1985) ended the "fleeing felon rule" that had provided the legal basis for most of these shootings. The decision limited police use of deadly force to situations where the officer or others were facing the threat of serious physical harm. However, the experience in the 1992 Los Angeles riots demonstrated that looting can be contained without the use of deadly force. The lesson is that looters respond rationally to police activity. In the LA neighborhoods where the police maintained a presence, looting never began; in neighborhoods where looting had started, once arrests of looters began, the looting ended. Media coverage of police standing by while looting occurred guaranteed its rapid spread. Cannon notes "Television spread the contagion of the looting . . . thousands of . . . people could see that looters were unopposed by the police, and they rushed to join in the pillaging" (Cannon 1999, p. 338).

In racially charged situations, public leaders may be reluctant to use a strong police presence to deter looting. The concern is that the presence of the police may lead to more violence, and thus giving in to looting may be the lesser of two evils. Oakland Mayor Ron Dellums, commenting on the looting stemming from the rioting after the death of Oscar Grant, described the trashed businesses as the "cost of democracy" (MacDonald 2010). Dellums said: "If you embrace the reality of people's legitimate rights and step back, then things are going to happen. Some people will exploit that openness" (MacDonald 2010). To Dellums, "stepping back" meant no real police protection for the businesses vandalized by looters.

The same dynamic may have been in play in Ferguson. Prior to the release of the grand jury report on the Brown shooting, Ferguson officials asked Governor Nixon to deploy National Guard troops to protect local businesses. Nixon pledged to use the National Guard, but as violence and looting broke out, the troops remained in their barracks. Nixon's failure to deploy the troops became a major issue in Missouri, with legislative leaders demanding answers (Young 2014).

The comments on looting during the Baltimore rioting in April 2015 by public officials, including President Obama, suggest a hardening of attitude toward looters. The mayor of Baltimore, Stephanie Rawlings-Blake, originally described the destruction as "idiotic" and referred to looters as "thugs" (Fang 2015). She backed off those comments a day later via Twitter, but Obama took a harder tone. The president also referred to the looters as "thugs." In commenting on the riots, he said,

> There's no excuse for the kind of violence that we saw yesterday. It is counterproductive. When individuals get crowbars and start prying open doors to loot, they're not protesting. They're not making a statement. They're stealing. When they burn down a building, they're committing arson. And they're destroying and undermining businesses and opportunities in their own communities. That robs jobs and opportunity from people in that area. (Bradner 2015)

Looting during riots remains a difficult challenge for the police. Although many people view looting as a misdemeanor theft offense, under most state criminal law, it is a felony. Looters enter a premises by force to commit a crime, and that constitutes felony burglary. Adequate personnel and lower levels of force can deter looting. The level of force police should use in response to looting would constitute a productive community discussion.

Riots and Corruption of the Justice System

In Elaine, Arkansas, after the riot in 1919, the criminal justice system became a cudgel used against the black community. African American defendants accused of murder and a variety of other charges received minimal legal assistance, and they were quickly convicted by all-white juries. Only the intervention of the NAACP and skillful attorneys working on behalf of the defendants prevented gross miscarriages of justice.

The country has changed significantly since 1919, and although many might find it comfortable to embrace the narrative of blind justice, the facts speak otherwise. A review of riot history shows multiple examples of how the threat of rioting influences the criminal justice process.

After the not guilty verdict in the state trial of the LAPD officers involved in the King beating led to horrific riots, jurors in the later federal trial of the officers were very aware of the potential of their decision to spark more violence. The federal prosecutors had presented a strong case against the officers, "but their greatest success in the jury room lay in reminding jurors about the deadly riots that had engulfed Los Angeles less than a year earlier—and arousing fears of more to come" (Cannon 1999, p. 473). In fact, one writer noted, "Fear, in fact, was the thirteenth juror" in the federal King case (Cannon 1999, p. 475).

The BART shooting and subsequent disorder in Oakland illustrates the power of threatened rioting to affect court proceedings. After Officer Johannes Mehserle was found guilty of involuntary homicide, rioting broke out. Protesters believed the two- to four-year sentence was too lenient, and prosecutors pushed use of a "gun specification" provision to enhance the prison sentence Mehserle might face. Gun specification laws were passed to provide additional deterrent to criminals using guns during robberies and other violent offenses. The use of this provision to provide additional punishment for Mehserle, who carried a gun as a sworn police officer, would have been "redundant and illogical" according to Stanford University Law Professor Robert Weisberg. In a nice piece of understatement, Weisberg added, "this is an odd application of the statute" (Elias and Risling 2010).

The purpose of adding the gun specification had little to do with rational sentencing and was more about fear of rioting. A news story on the sentencing made officials' intent crystal clear. "But since the jury also found Mehserle used a gun during the crime, the judge could tack on an additional three to 10 years—an option Oakland officials hope would quell additional unrest in the city" (Elias and Risling 2010).

In some cases, fear of rioting tainted some officials' comments and threatened the integrity of an investigation. Just days after the Brown shooting and long before any serious investigation could possibly have been completed, Missouri Governor Jay Nixon stated "a vigorous prosecution must now be pursued." He added, "We have a responsibility to come together, and do everything we can to achieve justice for [Brown's] family" (FoxNews.com 2014). Statements like Nixon's serve little purpose but to throw a match into a combustible situation; they certainly do violence to any rational investigative process.

Police Slowdowns and Increased Violence

The aftermath of riots brings a change in police behavior, a withdrawal from active policing, and a subsequent increase in community violence. Officers begin to avoid confrontations that have the potential for use of force, fearing lawsuits, departmental discipline, job loss, and worse. LAPD Sergeant Tim Day explained it this way: "An officer can go down an alley where the gangsters hang out or he can go down a main street where nothing is happening. Why would you go down the alley when the public doesn't seem to support you for your efforts?" (Cannon 1999, pp. 545–46). After the 1992 riots, LAPD officers began to practice what they referred to as "drive and wave" policing—doing little proactively and responding only to 911 calls. As crime increased, arrests in LA dropped by over a third (from 1981 to 1995). As expressed by an experienced LAPD detective, "the city does not want its police officers to be involved in violent activity, so police are not putting themselves in situations where violence may occur" (Cannon 1999, p. 545).

A similar process played out in Cincinnati. After the riots in 2001, violent crime escalated dramatically. In the three years following the riots, homicides more than doubled. Yet police activity dropped by nearly every measure. From the year prior to the riots compared to the year after, drug arrests dropped by a third, other vice arrests dropped by 40 percent, and traffic enforcement declined by 50 percent (Cincinnati Police Division 2003).

Violence also surged in the aftermath of the Baltimore riots. Following the riots in April 2015, May 2015 became the deadliest month in Baltimore in fifteen years, with thirty-eight homicides reported. Of those, ten occurred in the Western District, the neighborhood where the April rioting was centered. Nonfatal shootings also escalated in the Western District of the city, with ninety-one shootings recorded in May alone (Linderman 2015).

As in Los Angeles in 1992 and Cincinnati in 2001, the Baltimore violence was accompanied by a sharp decrease in policing activity. Arrests by Baltimore police in May were down over 50 percent, and the sentiments expressed by Baltimore police officers echo the comments by LAPD officers twenty-five years earlier. Anthony Batts, the police commissioner, said that officers fear being arrested if they make a mistake. The result is a police withdrawal from a community most in need of effective policing.[3]

Statistics paint only part of the picture. Community residents living in fear of violence pay a much higher price. One Baltimore resident, Antoinette Perrine, told a reporter, "I'm afraid to go outside. People wake up with shots through their windows" (Linderman 2015). Since the riots, Perrine barricades her door and has installed metal plates inside the windows to protect her from gunfire.

Another Baltimore resident eloquently captured the results of depolicing. "Now there's no police. People feel as though they can do things and get away with it. I see people walking with guns almost every single day, because they know the police aren't pulling them up like they used to" (Linderman 2015).

Discussion

The price paid by US communities in the aftermath of rioting provides a clear signal that riot prevention should be a priority for public officials. Riots represent a failure in governance, yet there is a reluctance to even discuss the possibility. Part of the reluctance comes from the tension that continues to exist around race relations in this country. It is a difficult and uncomfortable topic for citizens of every race. Yet avoidance of the issue increases a community's risk for disorder. Many public and police leaders share the view of some authorities in cities previously victimized by rioting that even discussion of the issue might be seen as provocation.

In fact, open and full discussion of riot prevention can provide an immunization effect for a community. These discussions, with as broad of a swath of the community as possible, can open the door to a new type of relationship between the community and the police that will not only reduce the risk of rioting but put the police on the path as true community partners in reducing crime and disorder.

As the major issue dividing police and the community, use of force must be the number one priority in opening the community discussion. Police force policy, force options used by the police, training, the investigative process when force incidents occur, and the role of race in these incidents should all be part of the conversation.

Notes

1. In my own experience, written tests tell little about one's potential for effective police performance. This is true for both entry and promotional tests. It is generally recognized in police departments that good test-takers are not necessarily good officers or supervisors.

2. For more information on external oversight of police, the National Association for Civilian Oversight of Law Enforcement (NACOLE) is an excellent resource. See https://nacole.org/.

3. In multiple speeches in late 2015, FBI Director James Comey described "a Ferguson effect," stating police officers in cities experiencing racial disorder were withdrawing from active policing, resulting in increased violent crime. As the brief history in this chapter illustrates, this phenomenon predates Ferguson.

5

Police Use
of Force

*While force is the core of the police role, the skill in policing consists
of finding ways to avoid its use.*

—Egon Bittner

*When the police chief is called at 3:30 in the morning and told
"Chief, one of our cops has just shot a kid," the chief's first questions
are: "What color is the cop? What color is the kid?" And, the reporter
asked, if the answer is "The cop is white, the kid black?"*

"He gets dressed," replied Bouza.

—Anthony Bouza, former Minneapolis police chief

Racial tensions are most acute in the aftermath of a police
force incident. The death of an African American at the hands of the
police, particularly a white officer, provides a test of community and
police leadership. When the fallout from these events results in disorder and rioting, the damage done echoes for years in racial tension,
increased violence, and a fraying of the community fabric. The community conversation following police force, particularly deadly force
incidents, often inflames rather than informs and provides a graphic
demonstration of the gap between police and the people they serve.
The tension largely stems from a deep-seated distrust of the police in

the black community, a distrust engendered by "many years of silent decisions and corrosive behavior that tarnished and destroyed the trust of a people in law enforcement" (Cincinnati Enquirer 2015, p. 6A).

A focus on transparent policing that builds a strong foundation for police legitimacy is the clearest path to mending the racial rift. Key to this effort is a shared understanding of the complexity of force issues, including the legal parameters for use of force, the investigative process of these incidents, and the difficult conversation on the role of race in police use of force incidents.[1]

Legal Issues in Police Use of Force

On October 2, 1974, at 11 p.m., two Memphis police officers received a radio dispatch for a prowler. Officers Elton Hymon and Leslie Wright had no idea this routine call would lead to a landmark Supreme Court decision on police deadly force.

The officers were met by a woman who told them she had heard breaking glass and believed someone had broken into the house next door. Hymon started to the rear of the house and Wright remained out front. As he reached the back of the house, Hymon heard a door slam and witnessed a figure running through the backyard. There was a fence across the back of the property, and the suspect hesitated at the fence. Hymon drew his service revolver, shone his flashlight on the suspect, and shouted at the suspect to stop. Hymon did not observe any weapon and later described the suspect as 5'5" to 5'7" and seventeen or eighteen years old. The suspect crouched momentarily at the base of the fence, and Hymon again shouted "Police! Halt!" The suspect began climbing the fence. Believing that if the suspect got over the fence he would get away, Hymon fired a single shot, hitting the suspect in the head and killing him.

The deceased was Edward Garner, a fifteen-year-old Memphis eighth-grader. Garner had ransacked the house, taking cash. Hymon's use of deadly force was allowable under a 1974 Tennessee state law, which read: "If, after notice of the intention to arrest the defendant, he either flees or forcibly resists, the officer may use all the necessary means to effect the arrest" (*Tennessee v. Garner*, 471 US 1, 1985).

Garner's family sued for excessive use of force, and the case took eleven years to reach the Supreme Court. In its ruling, the Supreme Court set a new constitutional standard for police use of deadly force.

The court reasoned when police use deadly force to apprehend someone, it is constitutionally a "seizure" and therefore falls under the
Fourth Amendment, which prohibits "unreasonable search and
seizure" by the government. Much of the argument before the court
considered whether police had the right to use deadly force against
fleeing suspects, including burglary offenders like Garner. The discussion revolved around the constitutionality of the "fleeing felon"
rule, under which police could use deadly force to stop suspects running from a felony offense.

The Court agreed that although burglary was a serious offense,
that fact alone did not justify the use of deadly force in the Garner
case. The Court noted that Hymon did not perceive any danger to
himself from Garner. Hymon testified he shot Garner only to prevent
his escape. The Court reasoned that while Hymon certainly had probable cause to arrest Garner, it was unreasonable and unconstitutional
to use deadly force simply to make the arrest. The court decided the
fleeing felon rule, on its face, was unconstitutional, and thus police
would no longer be legally able to use deadly force simply to stop a
suspect running from a felony. In setting the new standard, the court
said an officer may use deadly force only if "he has probable cause to
believe that the suspect poses a threat of serious physical harm either
to the officer or to others" (*Tennessee v. Garner*).

The standard articulated in the Garner decision applied only to
deadly force situations. Four years after this decision, the Supreme Court
used the *Connor v. Graham* case to expand the Fourth Amendment standard of "reasonableness" to all uses of police force (*Graham v. Connor*,
490 US 386, 1989).

The Graham case stemmed from an incident in Charlotte, North
Carolina. On the evening of November 12, 1984, Dethorne Graham, a
diabetic, felt the onset of what he described as a "sugar attack." He
asked his friend Wilford Berry to drive him to a nearby convenience
store where he could get some orange juice.

On their arrival, Berry stayed in the car while Graham entered
the store looking for some juice. Seeing long check-out lines, Graham
decided against buying anything, left the store, jumped back in the
car with Berry, and told him to drive to a nearby friend's house.
Charlotte Police Officer M. S. Conner was parked across the street,
and Graham's quick entrance and exit from the store caught his attention. Conner followed Berry's car out of the lot and stopped him
about half a mile from the store. When Connor approached the driver,

Berry explained Graham's need for juice. Connor told the pair to remain in the car and radioed for another officer to check the store and confirm that nothing had happened.

As Connor returned to the police car, Graham got out of Berry's car, ran around it twice, sat down on the curb, and then passed out. Other officers arrived. One rolled Graham over and handcuffed him. There was some discussion among the officers on what might be wrong with Graham. One officer was particularly vehement that diabetes was not the issue. "I've seen a lot of people with sugar diabetes that never acted like this. Ain't nothing wrong with the M.F. but drunk" (*Graham v. Connor*).

Officers lifted Graham up and placed him face down on the hood of the car. He regained consciousness and told officers he had a card in his wallet verifying that he had diabetes. An officer told him to shut up and shoved his face against the hood of the car. A friend of Graham's showed up at the scene and offered him some orange juice. Officers refused to let Graham have the juice.

A few minutes later, Connor received a radio notification from an officer at the store verifying there had been no offense. Graham was uncuffed, given his juice, and sent on his way.

Graham suffered some significant injuries during his rough handling by the police. He had a bruised forehead, cuts on his wrists, a shoulder injury, and a broken foot. He sued for excessive use of force and the case made its way to the Supreme Court in 1989.

The Court ruled they were extending the reasonableness standard established in the Garner case to police nondeadly force incidents. "Today, we make explicit what was implicit in Garner's analysis, and hold that all claims that law enforcement officers have used excessive force—deadly or not—in the course of an arrest, investigatory stop, or other 'seizure' of a free citizen should be analyzed under Fourth Amendment and its 'reasonableness' standard" (*Graham v. Connor*).

The court identified four factors to apply in each case to determine whether a particular use of force is reasonable. The factors were: the severity of the crime at issue, whether the suspect poses an immediate threat to the safety of the officers or others, whether he is actively resisting, and whether he is attempting to evade arrest by flight. These factors allow for a determination "whether the totality of circumstances justifies a particular sort of . . . seizure" (*Graham v. Connor*).

Probably the most important point made by the Supreme Court in *Graham* was allowing police officers a substantial degree of latitude in making use of force judgments. Specifically, the Court said, "The 'reasonableness' of a particular use of force must be judged from the perspective of a reasonable officer on the scene, and its calculus must embody an allowance for the fact that police officers are often forced to make split-second decisions about the amount of force necessary in a particular situation" (*Graham v. Connor*).

The most crucial elements detailed in the two Supreme Court decisions are:

- Deadly force may not be used unless the officer has probable cause to believe the suspect poses a significant threat of death or serious physical harm to the officer or others.
- Use of force, including deadly force decisions, should be judged under the Fourth Amendment reasonableness standard.
- The reasonableness standard is not subject to precise definition or mechanical application.
- Each situation must be viewed from the point of view of a reasonable officer on the scene, accounting for the totality of circumstances.
- Reasonableness must account for the fact that police officers make use-of-force decisions "in circumstances that are tense, uncertain, and rapidly evolving" (*Graham v. Connor*).

Courts have given significant deference to officer judgment in force incidents. In *Scott v. Hendrich* (39 F 3rd 912 [9th Cir. 1994]), a deadly force case in which plaintiffs argued the officer could have used a less lethal force method, the federal appeals court noted, "as long as the police use of deadly force was reasonable, the constitution does not require them to use less intrusive alternatives." In *Plakas v. Drinski* (19 F. 3rd 1143 [7th Cir. 1994]), the court specifically warned against second-guessing of police in force situations. "We do not return to prior segments of the event and, in the light of hindsight, reconsider whether prior police decisions were correct."

Controversy surrounding these events often revolves around differing perceptions of the threat faced by an officer. FBI legal instructor John Hall notes, "What is often disputed is an officer's assessment of a threat and the level of force selected to counter it. As a general principle, the level of force used should be tailored to the nature of the threat that prompted it" (Hall 1992, p. 22).

Force Options

Presence

Police are equipped with a variety of options when confronted with a force situation. The most obvious is the simple physical presence of the officer, in uniform with a badge and firearm. Citizens are expected to comply with orders from a police officer, and in the overwhelming majority of police–citizen contacts, compliance occurs without any issue. Police trainers invest significant energy in developing *command presence* in police recruits, in the belief the demeanor and bearing of the officer are key factors in securing voluntary compliance. Command presence speaks to professionalism and competence in a manner that also conveys respect and dignity.

> When a police officer arrives on the scene, everyone there begins to take his measure. His physical presence, his verbalizations, the things he says and does in that first few seconds can dramatically alter the dynamics of the situation. The officer's reading of the situation and his response can defuse the potential for violence or in some cases, act as a spark in an explosive atmosphere. (Rahtz 2003)

Courtesy and empathy are two crucial elements in every police–citizen encounter. Corporate communications expert Paul Meshanko notes that being treated with respect generates a "neurological response" that engenders cooperation (Meshanko 2013). Conversely, treating people in a demeaning or abusive fashion creates an emotional response likely to escalate the situation.

Although physical presence is the first force option, officers are equipped with a variety of other force tools. These options include mace or chemical irritant, tasers, batons, and deadly force options including handguns, shotguns, and patrol rifles. An understanding of the dynamics of these tools, their effectiveness, and policy regarding their use is a good starting point for engaging the community on police force issues.

Chemical Irritant

Chemical irritant (CI), more widely described as mace or pepper spray, is the most commonly used police force option. It is easy to use, allows officers to maintain some distance from combative people, and works well 90 percent of the time (Rahtz 2003, p. 48). Research found use of CI led to fewer assaults on officers and reduced injuries to officers and citizens (Rahtz 2003, p. 48). Further, a 2001 study by the International Association of Chiefs of Police documented that as police use of CI increased, police use of firearms decreased.

CI has its limitations. It is not a precise weapon, and in close proximity with or physically engaged with an aggressive person, the officer may also be affected by the spray. The spray takes several seconds for full effect on a person, and ideally, an officer can keep enough distance to give the CI a chance to work. There are no serious side effects, and water and/or a moving breeze acts as effective decontamination.

Over 97 percent of local police and 96 percent of sheriff's departments allow for use of CI by their officers (Dempsey and Forst 2013, p. 76).

Taser

Conducted energy devices (CEDs), or tasers, have quickly become a popular addition to the use-of-force arsenal. The taser was developed by Jack Cover, a NASA scientist who did research on nondeadly weapons in the 1960s. Cover gave his weapons the name TASER, an acronym for the Thomas A. Swift Electric Rifle, named after a popular children's adventure hero in the 1920s.

As of 2011, Cover's electric weapon (taser) was being used by 15,000 police agencies nationwide (Alpert et al. 2011). Despite its increasing popularity, widespread use of tasers by police has not been without controversy.

Amnesty International tracked taser-related deaths and reports between 2001 and 2008; more than 500 people in the United States have died after being tased (Trimel 2012). Autopsies confirm, in the overwhelming majority of cases, that victims had serious preexisting health conditions. Tasers work effectively and safely in the majority of cases. Per the National Institute of Justice (NIJ), "researchers found that 99.7 percent of people who were shocked by CEDs suffered no injuries or minor injuries only." In fact, the research concluded, "CED use actually decreases the likelihood of suspect injury" (Alpert et al. 2011).

The taser is obviously an effective tool. The more pressing policy issue is matching taser use with levels of resistance. Initial taser training provided to police agencies suggested the taser could be used for people exhibiting low levels of resistance, like verbal combativeness.[2] As tasers have been more widely deployed, many departments have limited their use to situations where an officer is facing active physical resistance (Miller 2010). One study found that a change in policy to limit the use of tasers to higher levels of aggression by citizens resulted in increased levels of suspect resistance and slightly increased officer injuries (Miller 2010).

Tasers are effective, but with significant limitations. The two barbs that carry the electric current from the weapon in the hand of a police officer to the individual must *both* strike the individual and embed themselves in or extremely close to the skin surface. The barbs optimally separate about twelve to eighteen inches before striking the individual. The effective deployment range on a taser is fifteen to eighteen feet, with a maximum range of twenty-one feet. If one barb strikes the individual but the second misses, the weapon will not work. If a person is wearing heavy clothing, preventing the barbs from penetrating close to the skin, the weapon will not work.

Deployment of tasers by police agencies has to be done with recognition of not only the initial costs but training, maintenance, and equipment expenses as well. Tasers are shaped like handguns, but despite the different feel and the color difference, there have been instances of weapons confusion—officers pulling their handgun believing it is their taser, leading to accidental shootings.[3] The 2009 BART shooting in Oakland and a 2015 police shooting in Tulsa were both linked to weapons confusion.

Baton

The police nightstick or baton remains a use-of-force tool in many police departments. The baton is the oldest of force tools. It was first put into use by British bobbies in the early 1800s and called a truncheon. Two hundred years later, the ubiquitous nightstick or baton is gradually disappearing from the police landscape. One reason is the addition of so many items to the police gun belt—gloves, radio, handcuffs, flashlight, pager, and cell phone, to name a few items—that space on the belt has become a priority. In response, some agencies are removing the baton from the officer's force options.

While the taser is a technological advancement, the baton is the least advanced option available to an officer. Training with batons distinguishes between "pain compliance" strikes, targeted at the back of the thigh or buttocks as an example, and blows meant to cause injury, targeted at a knee joint or elbow. Blows meant to cause injury would be considered a reasonable use of force when an officer is faced with a high level of resistance. Batons could also be considered deadly force when used to strike a person in the head.

The police baton is a primitive instrument. Despite the fancy nomenclature renaming them as "impact weapons," the bottom line is that they are wooden or metal clubs that human beings have been whacking each other with for thousands of years. A number of police agencies are relegating nightsticks to police museums.

Hand to Hand

Policing is a hands-on business. Officers are constantly separating people, restraining them with body weight, using escort holds to move them from place to place, and sometimes striking them. Skolnick and Fyfe (1993, p. 116) quote an active urban officer: "I can't think of a single day when I didn't put my hands on somebody."

The most frequent type of physical force used by police officers consists of low-level actions—pushing, pulling, restraining, and grabbing. Less frequently, officers may strike with a hand or fist, kick or knee, throw someone to the ground, or wrestle an individual. Police training includes pressure points, joint locks, upper body restraints, and ground fighting techniques as physical control measures.

Success in use of physical techniques is dependent on officer skills, training, and physical conditioning. The majority of officers are hardly in a league with martial artists like Steven Segal or Jackie Chan, and their odds of success in a physical confrontation with a person who is likely to be younger, stronger, and/or under the influence of drugs is questionable at best. Probably the biggest deterrent to officers becoming involved in physical fights with citizens is the fact that about 25 percent of the police officers killed each year are murdered with their own weapons (Brown and Langan 2001). From their first day at the academy, officers are reminded that every time they are in a hand-to-hand physical confrontation with a suspect, the confrontation involves a gun (the officer's weapon).

Firearms

A police officer's firearm is the ultimate deadly force option. In addition to the sidearm carried on a gun belt, officers are likely to have access to shotguns or patrol rifles. Those weapons may be stored in the trunk of the police car or secured in a rack inside the passenger compartment.

A department's policy on firearms may dictate the specific handgun officers may carry, may allow them to carry more than one handgun, may allow different weapons based on assignment (investigations versus patrol), or may give officers some choice in the selection of a handgun.

Departmental decisions and policy on firearms may have a serious impact on police use of force. In 1988, Washington DC police issued Glock 9 mm semi-automatic pistols to its officers. Among firearms experts, the Glock was known to have a sensitive trigger. A *Washington Post* investigation found the number of accidental discharges by DC police officers in 1994 exceeded both New York's and Chicago's, both much larger departments. Lack of training also was an issue. The investigation found that 75 percent of all DC officers involved in shootings in 1996 failed to comply with retraining regulations. One officer waited so long to come to the range that firearms instructors found a spider web growing inside his gun (Leen and Horwitz 1998, p. A-1).

Use of Force Decision Making

In a use-of-force situation, the challenge for police officers is to choose the most appropriate (reasonable) tool for the circumstances at hand. In providing guidance for officers in force situations, trainers and supervisors often utilize a use-of-force continuum. At its simplest, the continuum is a chart matching suspect actions with reasonable force options. Figure 5.1 is a simple continuum.

The Ohio Peace Officer Training Academy (OPATA), which certifies all Ohio police Officers, uses the use of force continuum found in Figure 5.2. That continuum also adds color-coding, signifying increasing danger from blue at the low end to red at the high end. The

Figure 5.1 Use-of-Force Continuum Resistance and Response Levels

Suspect Resistance Level	Officer Level of Force Control
Suspect presence	Interview stance
Verbal resistance	Verbal commands
Passive resistance	Transport techniques
Defensive resistance	Chemical agents
Active physical resistance	Physical tactics/Weapons
Firearms/deadly force	Firearms/deadly force

Source: Alport and Smith 1999.

chart attempts to match specific force options with suspect behavior. The LVNR on the chart stands for lateral vascular neck restraint, or what most observers would call a chokehold. Applying the LVNR requires the officer to place his arm around the neck of the suspect, elbow down, and squeeze the sides of the neck between the bicep and forearm. The pressure is not applied to the front of the neck, and if properly applied, it does not cut off the air supply. It does constrict the blood flow to the brain, causing unconsciousness.

While force continuums provide some guidance for police officers, even a cursory review shows them to be lacking. What the continuums attempt to describe, as precisely as possible, is what a reasonable officer would do in various situations. Yet as the Supreme Court noted in the *Graham* decision, "the test of reasonableness under the Fourth Amendment is not capable of precise definition or mechanical application" (*Graham v. Connor*, 490 US 386, 1989). Ultimately, the continuums fail to capture the host of factors involved in making use-of-force decisions.

Figure 5.2. Use-of-Force Continuum

Individual Action	Officer Response
Red Weapons used against officer; attempting to disarm officer; life-threatening, weaponless assault	Deadly force
Orange Striking or kicking officer	Baton techniques or LVNR
Yellow Wrestling with officer; pushing officer	Striking, punching, kicking, mace, teargas, or electrical device, baton restraint
Green Pulling away from officer; refusing to move—dead weight	Take downs, joint manipulations, striking muscle groups or masses
Blue Not responding to commands Verbal or physical danger clues	Balance displacement, escort Balance displacement, assistance from other officers, commands, officer presence

Consider the variation inherent in the simple phrase "officer presence." Are we referring to a physically imposing officer who looks like an NFL linebacker? Are we talking about an officer of any size who exudes competence and professionalism? Or are we talking about an officer whose demeanor suggests a hangover? Are we talking about an officer who is rude and overbearing, dismissive and arrogant? Common sense and research tells us the communication skills of officers can dramatically affect the outcome, for better or for worse, of all police–citizen encounters.

Despite the complexity, there are some general guidelines that provide a foundation for policy on use of force, training, and incident evaluation.

- Officers may use only that level of force that is reasonably necessary and no more. What is reasonable will be based on the individual situation and the various factors involved. Although it is difficult to define, "reasonable" covers a lot of territory.
- The reasonableness of the force used will reflect not only the amount of resistance encountered but also factors related to the officer and citizen involved. In the wording of the Supreme Court, the incident will be judged on the "totality of circumstances." Good officers, with training and experience, will be able to clearly articulate these factors.
- Officer action is *not* dictated solely by suspect behavior. Suspect behavior obviously is a major factor limiting officer alternatives, but officers always have some decision making to do. Even the worst-case gunfights will involve decisions on cover, concealment, and choice of weapons (Rahtz 2003, p. 65).

Use-of-Force Policy

Can a use-of-force policy effectively control officer behavior on the street? The evidence suggests that policy does have a significant effect. Research dating back to the 1980s found police use of deadly force was heavily influenced by organizational philosophies, expectations, and policies (Skolnick and Fyfe 1993).

One study reviewed deadly force data in Philadelphia following the removal of a restrictive policy in 1974 and the reinstatement of the restrictive policy in 1980. The study concluded that administrative policy can be an effective factor controlling police use of deadly force (White 2001).

In reviewing those studies, another author concluded,

> the effectiveness of administrative policy is less related to the policy itself than to the organizational context surrounding it. A use of force policy, no matter how elegantly crafted, that is implemented without significant organization support is unlikely to have much impact on officer behavior. Conversely, a sound policy, supported by ongoing training, enforced by effective supervision and communicated by a committed management team will not only control officer use of force but enhance officer safety and tactical practices as well. (Rahtz 2003, p. 95)

Designing an effective use-of-force policy relies on at least two important decisions. The first is constructing a policy clearly defining use of force. At what level of force should policy come into play? As noted, police officers are routinely grabbing, pushing, and restraining people. Should a policy identify these events as police use-of-force incidents? Should it require them to be reported and included in agency statistics? Should these incidents require an investigation as to their reasonableness? The practicality of counting these types of minor force precludes their inclusions in any serious policy, but the question remains as to exactly where should the line be drawn. Most force policies require supervisor notification and reporting on any use of weapons by officers—mace, baton, taser, punch, kick, or other body blow. Most also require any citizen injury as a result of police action to be followed by supervisor notification and reporting. A sprained wrist as a result of short physical struggle is an example.

The second major policy issue is the level and intensity of the force investigation. When deadly force is used, a criminal investigation follows. These investigations follow the same protocol and process that every homicide investigation entails. Where police force results in the death of a citizen, other investigations follow. The civilian oversight bodies found in some jurisdictions may conduct an independent investigation. The internal investigations department will follow the homicide investigation with additional scrutiny, focusing on administrative and criminal violations. The local prosecutor may conduct their own investigation for presentation to the grand jury. In some cases, as in Ferguson in 2014, the federal Department of Justice may do their own investigation.

While the intensive and multilayered investigations that accompany a police-related death are a given, the level of investigations for a taser usage, a mace incident, or other lesser force incident should be specified as part of agency policy. Photos; review of any police or other video available; statements by officers, witnesses, and citizens involved; and any physical evidence can be included. As the seriousness of the incident escalates, the intensity of the investigation should also increase.

From a policy standpoint, there is no standard national definition of police use of force, nor any recognized single standard for investigation of these incidents. Department policies should all adhere to the constitutional standards articulated in *Tennessee v. Garner* and *Graham v. Connor*, but beyond that, the construction of a comprehensive policy is in the hands of local police officials.[4] The President's Task Force on 21st Century Policing (Final Report, p. 19) contains a number of recommendations for development of use-of-force policy.

The Role of Race

The intersection of race and use of force is the most contentious issue separating police and the black community. Police racism—from police-sanctioned violence against black citizens to neglect of crime problems in black neighborhoods—is one of the most shameful chapters in US policing history. Police action and in some cases nonaction are clearly major factors in race rioting. Police were the enforcers of Jim Crow and were prominent in the sometimes brutal response to civil rights marches in the 1960s. Whereas other minority groups have complaints about discriminatory policing, the issue is most vivid for African Americans. Bluntly put, is the behavior of police officers—from stop and frisk practices, to traffic stops, to the use of force—influenced by racial factors?

In a 1995 summary of the research, Locke noted, "What every single study of police use of *fatal* force has found is that persons of color (principally black males) are a disproportionately high number of the persons shot by police compared to their representation in the general population. Where the studies diverge are the reasons for such disproportionality" (Locke 1995, p. 140). A 1998 study of police shootings in 170 large US cities found that racial inequality and a city's violent crime rates were causal factors in police killings of African Americans (Jacobs and O'Brien 1998). The racial gap has narrowed since the 1960s when African Americans were fatally shot by the police at a rate six times that of whites. That reported disparity was cut in half by the late 1980s.

However, recent reports have thrown the accuracy of much of the data on police shootings into question. Although the FBI provides an annual report on officer-involved shootings, there is no requirement for police departments to report these deaths. Beginning in 2015, the *Washington Post* began tracking fatal police shootings. They documented 385 fatal police shootings through the first five months of the year, a rate nearly double that reported to the FBI. Of the 385 deaths tracked by the *Post*, 46 percent were white and 27 percent were black (Kindy and Kimbriell 2015). If that number is accurate and adjusting for population, the ratio of black citizens killed by the police to white citizens killed by the police remains close to the federal figures from the late 1980s.

For black citizens, the debate over the extent of bias in policing is personal. Historian Henry Louis Gates Jr. captured the personal nature of biased policing in his writing for *New Yorker* magazine. "Blacks—in particular, black men—swap their experiences of police encounters like war stories, and there are few who don't have more than one story to tell" (Gates 1997, pp. 151–52). David Harris, an Ohio attorney who has researched and written on racial profiling, notes: "It is virtually impossible to find black people who do not feel that they have experienced racial profiling. These experiences have a deep psychological and emotional impact on the individuals involved, and they also have a significant connection to many of the most basic problems in criminal justice and race" (Harris 1999, p. 269).

Most African Americans would laughingly dismiss the notion that policing is bias-free. History, as much as current practice, continues to color the interaction between police and African Americans. Randall Kennedy, author of *Race, Crime, and the Law*, notes that for the black community, the belief is that police tend to act more like a repressive force rather than public servants working to protect and serve. "Fueling this perception substantially supported in fact, that at least in part for racial reasons police tended to behave in a distinctively rude, overbearing, contemptuous fashion" (Kennedy 1997, p. 115).

Discussion

As the most explosive factor in the uneasy relationship between African Americans and the police, use of force should be a focal point of the effort to repair that relationship. A primary police effort in this area has been the Citizen Police Academy.[5] These programs, sponsored by local police agencies, walk volunteer participants through a variety of police-related topics, including use of force. The discussion often includes a session using a firearms training simulator (FATS). The FATS training puts the student in the position of a police officer confronted with a force scenario by video. Typically, the FATS training is experienced by participants as a powerful and realistic look at the complexity of police force.

The potential of such training for opening up discussion with community leaders was captured by the experience of Houston Black Panther Party leader Quanell X. Described as Houston's Al Sharpton, Quanell was a highly visible and vocal critic of the police. The Missouri City Police Department, just outside of Houston, invited Quanell to take part in some of their FATS and scenario-based training. After unloading numerous rounds on an unarmed man in a mock traffic stop, Quanell described the experience as "eye-opening" (Kaye 2015).

A program like Citizens Police Academy represents only a sliver of the potential in opening up a broader community conversation on use of force. The conversation should be designed to include a representation of the most skeptical slice of the community with a focus on African American youth. The President's Task Force Report on 21st Century Policing includes the recommendation "to affirm and recognize the voices of youth in community decision making, facilitate youth-led research and problem solving, and develop and fund youth leadership training and life skills through positive youth/police collaboration and interactions."

One example following the task force recommendation would be a youth leadership camp focusing on collaborative police and youth problem solving on use of force issues. The program could include scenario training exercises and be an opportunity to bridge the racial gap. Many police agencies offer summer camps with a typical menu of camp activities. The goal is providing a positive experience for youth interacting with police officers. The proposed camp would include that goal and substitute challenging work on force issues for some of the canoeing, swimming, and other activities.

While outreach to African American youth is a priority, the conversation on force issues needs to be much wider, with a specific effort to gain sponsorship and support from the black community. A police partnership with the NAACP or Urban League in sponsoring a police summit would be a good way to begin addressing concerns on both force and police bias. Topics could include the drug war, mass incarceration, police diversity, traffic stops, the citizen complaint process, and others. The particular topics are less important than the group process that occurs. Just the open discussion between police officers and community members will provide dividends for both with a significant build-up in police equity.

The choice of force options allowed for officers has serious consequences. In Los Angeles in the early 1980s, LAPD officers using chokeholds became a major issue. The chokehold referred to was what LAPD trainers described as "upper body control" or lateral vascular neck restraint (LVNR). As described earlier, when properly applied, LVNR cuts off blood supply to the brain, causing temporary unconsciousness. Following the deaths of African American citizens after chokeholds used by the LAPD, Chief Daryl Gates defended the technique, claiming "blacks had arteries that do not open up as fast as on normal people" (Duke 2010). In the ensuing uproar over Gates's comments, the police commission put the chokeholds on par with deadly force.[6]

Retired LAPD Captain Greg Meyer noted, "Following the banning of LVNR, there was an upsurge in baton use by LAPD officers." Chief Gates had warned the police commission that without the LVNR, increased baton use "would result in injury in almost every case, a result which does not occur from employment of upper-body control holds" (Meyer 2015). Gates's prediction was accurate. A year later, he reported to the police commission that injuries to suspects had risen 661 percent, and injuries to officers had risen 521 percent since the LVNR moratorium (Meyer 2015).

After the videotaped King beating in 1991, some LAPD trainers, including Myers, believed banning of the LVNR contributed to the high number of baton strikes administered to King. The LVNR remains a use-of-force option for a number of departments, including the Las Vegas Police Department, whose use-of-force policy is considered a national model.

Issuing any weapon to a police officer comes with the responsibility by the officer and the department to ensure appropriate equipment and adequate training. The 2009 BART shooting in Oakland is one example of what has come to be called "weapons confusion." Meyer has identified multiple instances nationwide where officers believed they were using a taser but shot a citizen with their handgun. The major factors in weapons confusion incidents include inadequate training and poor equipment (holster) choices. Myers notes most officers complete an eight-hour taser training program that may involve a limited number of practice shots. Yet most officers spend countless hours in training drawing and shooting their handgun. In some of the weapons confusion incidents, it appears that under stress, officer muscle memory reverts to the handgun.

Holster configuration also contributes to the problem. Some department policies place the taser and gun in close proximity, often on the same side of the body—right for right-handers and left for left-handers. Meyer says, "You've got to get the Taser away from the handgun. I've even gone so far as to recommend that the Taser be placed on the holster on the opposite side of the handgun, so it's accessible with the officer's weak hand. The strong hand is for your handgun, weak hand is for your Taser" (Stroud 2015).

The latest weapons confusion incident was the April 15, 2015, fatal shooting of a suspect by seventy-three-year-old Reserve Sheriff's Deputy Robert Bates in Tulsa, Oklahoma. Witnesses report just prior to the shot, Bates yelled, "Taser!" His immediate reaction following the shooting was "Oh! I shot him. I'm sorry!" (Stroud 2015). Bates has been charged with second-degree manslaughter, and the case is pending.

Although weapons confusion is the most serious of issues surrounding taser deployment, a recent court decision by the Fourth Circuit Court of Appeals narrows the legal use of tasers by the police.[7] Police in Pinehurst, NC, were attempting to take a mentally ill man to the hospital. The man wrapped himself around a stop sign post, refusing orders to let go. An officer placed his taser against the man, briefly shocking him, but despite five uses of the taser, the man would not let go of the post. Three officers finally pried the man off the pole, and he was forcibly handcuffed. After he was finally handcuffed, the man stopped breathing and died. In a suit filed against the officers, the court ruled the use of taser against this person was unconstitutional, as he was not a threat to anyone other than himself. The court noted, "Law enforcement officers should now be on notice that such taser use violates the Fourth Amendment" (Woolverton 2016).

The search for the perfect use-of-force tool is ongoing. The phaser, set on stun and popularized in *Star Trek*, has not yet been invented. Although the taser holds promise, its use has limitations, and the concerns over its safety have led some police departments to withdraw tasers from their officers.

Former Navy Seal Kenneth Stethem has developed an intermediate force tool that begins to close the technology gap. Stethem's tool, named the Mark 63 Trident, contains weapons including a high-intensity light, pepper spray, and a stun device. The high-intensity light is a unique addition because it causes a disorienting effect when used on a suspect.[8] Because the Mark 63 is several weapons in one device, Stethem says, "It shortens the decision matrix" (O'Neil 2011).

Colerain Township Police Department, in southwest Ohio, has provided the Mark 63 to all its officers. It replaced the separate taser and chemical irritant they formerly carried. Colerain Chief Dan Meloy said, "Once I saw it and saw the training I knew it was the right thing" (O'Neil 2011).

The search for better force technology continues. Use of force expert Greg Meyer put the challenge eloquently when he noted, "If we can put a man on the moon and return him safely to earth, why can't we put a man on the ground and take him safely to jail?" (Meyer 1993). Despite technology that has changed nearly every aspect of US life, police officers are still wrestling, punching, restraining, hitting with batons, spraying with mace, and shooting people.

Policing remains a face-to-face, person-to-person business. A calm demeanor and superior communications skills remain the number one safeguard for police and the people they encounter. Police officers are thrust into situations that demand the wisdom of Solomon but without time to consider the alternatives. At the same time, community expectations and public scrutiny of police actions are at an all-time high. The challenge for police leaders and the community is the selection, training, and support for officers that perform without bias and with compassion and competence.

Notes

1. For a more complete examination of force issues, see Rahtz (2003).

2. At the time Cincinnati police provided taser training to its officers, I was assigned to the CPD Police Academy and participated in the initial training provided by TASER, International.

3. To avoid weapons confusion, the taser should look and feel very different from a handgun. The bright yellow coloring applied to some taser models is a good idea.

4. The Las Vegas Police Department's use-of-force policy has been promulgated as a good model. It can be accessed at http://www.lvmpd.com/Portals/0/OIO/GO-008-15_UseofForce.pdf.

5. I organized and coordinated several citizen police academies during my tenure as Cincinnati Police Academy commander.

6. Greg Meyer, a use-of-force expert retired from LAPD, believes the deaths attributed to chokeholds were caused by positional asphyxia combined with the practice of "hog-tying" combative suspects.

7. The January 16, 2016, taser decision by the Fourth Circuit applies to officers in North Carolina, South Carolina, Maryland, Virginia, and West Virginia.

8. Stethem says the Mark 63 was inspired by the death of his brother, US Navy diver Robert Stethem, who was killed by Hezbulloh terrorists on TWA flight 947 in 1985.

6

The War on Drugs

America's public enemy number one in the United States is drug abuse. In order to fight and defeat this enemy, it is necessary to wage a new, all-out offensive.
—Richard Nixon, June 17, 1971

African Americans are not significantly more likely to use or sell prohibited drugs than whites, but they are made criminals at drastically higher rates for precisely the same conduct.

—Michelle Alexander, *The New Jim Crow*

For nearly fifty years, the United States has waged what is commonly described as the War on Drugs. Despite the money spent (over $1 trillion), millions of citizens incarcerated, and thousands more killed in drug-related violence, the drug problem is, by nearly any metric, more serious today than it was in 1970. The damage done includes mass incarceration of African Americans and an erosion of the constitutional protections enjoyed by all citizens. The War on Drugs is a major factor in the continuing schism between the police and the black community, corroding public safety and increasing the risk of rioting.

The War on Drugs

While President Richard Nixon initiated the War on Drugs, it was sub-sequently embraced and enlarged by both Republican and Democratic administrations. Over the years, drug policy became increasingly punitive as the country's leaders, in a nearly lock-step fashion, took a "tough on drugs" political stance.

In 1982, President Ronald Reagan declared, "We are going to win the War on Drugs." He put teeth in his promise by dramatically increasing funding for antidrug law enforcement efforts. In the early 1980s, funding for the DEA went from $86 million to $1,026 million, a tenfold increase. In similar fashion, the FBI antidrug budget went from $8 million to $95 million, and the Department of Defense antidrug allocation jumped from $33 million to $1,042 million. Reagan's emphasis on law enforcement was accompanied by a reduc-tion in federal funds directed toward drug treatment. The National Institute on Drug Abuse treatment funds and the support for the antidrug programs of the Department of Education were slashed by 80 percent (Alexander 2010, pp. 49–50).

Not to be outdone by his predecessor, in 1989, President George H. W. Bush succinctly stated his drug war policy, promising, "This scourge will stop." With congressional support, criminal penalties for small amounts of crack or base cocaine were greatly increased. Simple possession of crack cocaine, amounting to two sugar packs, brought a mandatory five-year minimum penalty for first offenders. This penalty was unprecedented in federal sentencing for drug offend-ers. Alexander points out: "Prior to 1988, one year of imprisonment had been the maximum for possession of any amount of any drug" (Alexander 2010, p. 54).

Those who believed the election of Bill Clinton would bring drug law reform were sorely mistaken. In 1992, Clinton escalated the rhet-oric, declaring, "President Bush hasn't fought a real war on crime and drugs. I will." This promise was part of a calculated move to steal the "tough on crime and drugs" issue away from the Republicans, and as president, Clinton was true to his word.

Clinton's crime policies resulted in a prison-building binge un-precedented in the United States. A 2008 Justice Policy Report tied his policies to "the largest increase in federal and state prison inmates of any president in American history" (Alexander 2010, p. 56). The majority of the growing prison population were drug offenders.

In defiance of federal policy, California approved medical marijuana in 1996. In a particularly frightening abuse of federal power, the Clinton administration Drug Enforcement Agency (DEA) reacted by instituting a series of SWAT-led drug raids on a number of California's legal marijuana dispensaries. Following the 1996 legalization, the DEA announced that any California doctors recommending medical marijuana to their patients would lose their DEA license (a necessity for medical practice) and face criminal charges. Federal action against the legal dispensaries included intimidation and bullying. Radley Balko notes that "in 2000, a federal judge chastised the Clinton administration for threatening doctors who even mentioned the benefits of medical marijuana to their AIDS and cancer patients" (Balko 2014, p. 215).

In the face of approval by California state voters of medical marijuana, federal drug enforcement faced a legal conundrum. As noted, the Clinton administration took a heavy-handed approach, arguing that federal law superseded state law. As other states followed California's lead, Clinton continued the policy of approving federal drug enforcement raids on legal marijuana facilities.

George W. Bush's election in 2000 brought more of the same. During the presidential campaign, Bush had promised a change in the policy, saying he would take a federalist position on medical marijuana, leaving the states to decide.

That promise died with Bush's election. "It quickly became clear that, like Clinton before him, Bush would give no quarter to sick people using pot in states that had legalized it for treatment" (Balko 2014, p. 252). Under Bush, the raids on medical marijuana dispensaries increased in intensity and numbers. The administration escalated the use of heavily armed police officers storming medical facilities and arresting staff and patients.[1]

With the election of Barack Obama in 2008, expectations rose again that real drug policy reform was in the offing. Obama had readily acknowledged drug use as a young man, including use of cocaine. In contrast to Clinton, who famously "did not inhale," in a 2005 speech Obama said, "I inhaled. Frequently. That was the point" (Harwell 2008).

The hope that Obama's administration would implement drug reform quickly faded. Once in office, Obama's administration accelerated federal police action against state-approved marijuana dispensaries. In his first four years, more federal raids on marijuana dispensaries were ordered than the Bush administration had undertaken in eight years (Balko 2014, p. 301).

Despite the federal effort, the number of states approving medical marijuana continued to increase. In February 2009, in the face of growing citizen support of medical marijuana, Attorney General Eric Holder announced that the federal government would no longer conduct raids on medical marijuana dispensaries in states where such dispensaries were legal. Holder's action ended the ugly spectacle of federal law enforcement storming legal medical facilities, arresting patients and medical staff.

Holder also announced his decision to terminate a long-standing tool of the War on Drugs: the civil asset forfeiture program. This action barred local and state police from using federal law to seize money and other assets from alleged drug dealers with no court finding that a crime has occurred. The program, a staple in antidrug law enforcement dating back to 1984, was a clear manifestation of the drug war's assault on the Bill of Rights.

Structured to allow police departments to keep cash and other assets seized from alleged drug offenders, local law enforcement suddenly had a financial incentive for active drug enforcement. Speaking to a journalist, DEA Agent William Ruzzamenti provided the following explanation of asset forfeiture in a case involving marijuana discovered on private farm land. The landowner insisted he had no knowledge of the grow operation. Ruzzamenti said, "Basically, people have to prove that they weren't involved and didn't know about it. Just the act of having marijuana grown on your land is enough to tie it up; then you have to turn around and prove you're innocent. *It reverses the burden of proof*" (Ray 1985, emphasis added, p. 105).

A 2014 case illustrates the reach of the asset forfeiture policy. In February 2014, Charles Clark, a student traveling from Orlando, Florida, was stopped by DEA agents at the Greater Cincinnati Airport. Baggage handlers had reported that his suitcase smelled of marijuana. Clark was stopped by a DEA agent, who found $11,000 in Clark's pants pocket. The cash was seized "upon probable cause that it was proceeds of drug trafficking or was intended to be used in an illegal drug transaction" (Pitcher 2015, p. 11a). Yet no drugs were found and no evidence was provided to support any reasonable belief that drug transactions of any kind were related to the money. Simply having a substantial amount of cash and the aroma of marijuana became reason enough for the government to seize the money. The burden was now on Clark to prove he came by the money outside the drug business.

Under the guise of drug enforcement, these types of seizures have become a common occurrence, with the federal government seizing $6.8 billion in citizen property between 2008 and 2013. In Clark's case, whether he was actually dealing drugs is immaterial to the seizure. The suspicion that he *might* be is enough, and the government seized his property without any criminal finding of guilt to any offense or even any criminal charges filed against him. To the War on Drugs machine, constitutional protections and due process are an inconvenience.

Despite the enormous expenditure of government funds and the incarceration of thousands of people, even a cursory review of drug war statistics shows a glaring public policy failure. The price and purity of illegal drugs, a metric by which the federal government measures its own success, have both moved in the wrong direction.

After nearly fifty years of the War on Drugs, overall addiction rates in the United States appear little different than they were in 1970, the year before Nixon declared the War on Drugs. Government reports estimated about 1.3 percent of Americans were addicted to drugs in 1970 (Kane 2004, p. 45). By the early 2000s, despite the cost in lives and dollars, the addiction rate remained at 1.3 percent (Robinson and Scherlen 2007, p. 94).The current opiate epidemic may have even increased this rate since 2000.

Drug use rates have remained largely unaffected by the prohibition regime. Specific use rates vary over time, and the emergence of a new drug (or an old one in new clothes) generally brings some changes in drug use choices. Heroin was the major drug of concern in the early days of the War on Drugs; the government was particularly concerned about the heavy use of heroin by troops in Vietnam, resulting in continuing addiction as the soldiers returned home.[2] Yet the addiction and use rate of Vietnam veterans after their return was no different than men who had not served in the military (Rahtz 2012, p. 85).

Crack cocaine became the major drug of concern in the 1980s and was largely replaced by methamphetamine in the 1990s. In recent years, the resurgence of heroin is a major concern, and the current heroin crisis is Exhibit A in the failure of drug prohibition. Despite a punitive approach dating to the early years of the War on Drugs, street heroin is now more available, cheaper, and of a higher potency than at any time since records have been kept (Salter and Caldwell 2010).

The Midwest portion of the country has been particularly hard hit. In Ohio, beginning in 2008, heroin/opiate overdoses have surpassed auto accidents as a cause of death. Heroin deaths in Ohio soared to over 2,100 in 2013, continuing a pattern of annual increases and a more than 10 percent jump from 2012 (Johnson and Candisky 2015).

Marijuana remains the country's most frequently used illegal drug, and despite the intensity of the penalties arrayed against it, its use continues to be a significant feature of US life. The statistics are persuasive. According to a study on marijuana policy released in 2015, thirty million Americans use marijuana each year; 42 percent of Americans have tried marijuana at least once; and over 30 percent of Americans used marijuana within the previous month (Marijuana Policies of Ohio Task Force 2015, p. 17). The report notes, "If marijuana prohibition laws in the United States . . . are intended to curtail marijuana use, research clearly demonstrates that they are at once extremely expensive and ineffective" (Marijuana Policies of Ohio Task Force 2015, p. 17).

Marijuana is now de facto legal in much of the country. Since 1996, twenty-two states have followed California in legalizing medical marijuana. Four other states plus Washington, DC, have legalized personal use of marijuana.

Despite the clear trend of social acceptance of marijuana, the government war on marijuana users goes on. Between 2001 and 2010, over eight million people were arrested for marijuana offenses. Eighty-eight percent of those arrests were for possession. Over that period, states spent an estimated $3.6 billion on marijuana possession offenses (ACLU 2013, p. 4).

If the War on Drugs could claim any positive results, or even demonstrate that its impact on citizens was minor, the effort to end it would be less urgent. Now, as the full extent of the harm related to drug prohibition emerges, the scale of the damage done to the African American community has become the most tragic chapter of the War on Drugs.

The Drug War and the Black Community

Racism has been a factor in drug prohibition efforts going back to the first antidrug law passed in the country. On November 15, 1875, San Francisco authorities made the operation of or presence in an opium den a misdemeanor crime. That ordinance was passed in the belief that opium use was being pushed by the Chinese to undermine US society.[3]

By the early 1900s, growing cocaine use drew the attention of policymakers. It was popularly believed cocaine use by African

Americans would provide them with super-human strength, making them "almost unaffected by mere .32 caliber bullets" (Musto 1987, p. 7). This fear of "cocainized Negroes" led a number of Southern police departments to move to .38-caliber weapons (Musto 1987, p. 7).

The federal Harrison Act of 1914, predecessor to modern antidrug legislation, was passed largely in part because of racist beliefs. Musto notes, "By 1914, prominent newspapers, physicians, pharmacists, and congressmen believed opiates and cocaine predisposed habitués toward insanity and crime. They were widely seen as substances associated with foreigners or alien subgroups. Cocaine raised the specter of the wild Negro, opium the devious Chinese, morphine the tramps in the slums" (Musto 1987, p. 65).

Marijuana was ignored by the Harrison Act, largely as a result of lobbying by the pharmaceutical industry, which viewed marijuana as a lucrative product. Not even those pushing the Harrison Act believed cannabis "was a problem of any major significance" (Musto 1987, p. 217).

Harry Anslinger had a different opinion. Anslinger was appointed head of the National Bureau of Narcotics in 1930, making him the country's first drug czar. He believed marijuana's effect on "the degenerate races" should make its prohibition a priority. Anslinger was rabidly racist, even in the context of his era, but his biases showed few boundaries. In speaking about marijuana users, Anslinger said, "There are 100,000 total marijuana smokers in the U.S., and most are Negroes, Hispanics, Filipinos and entertainers. Their Satanic music, jazz and swing result from marijuana use. This marijuana causes white women to seek sexual relations with Negroes, entertainers and any others."[4]

Anslinger falsified national drug use data to make it look as though the federal drug enforcement program under his leadership was a success. Through the 1930s, the Bureau of Narcotics published survey results showing dramatic declines in drug use. Later research found private correspondence from Anslinger admitting the numbers were a fabrication (Wing 2014). He maintained his position as the head of the Bureau of Narcotics until 1962.

Despite the major steps in civil rights and the undeniable progress in race relations over the past decades, race remains very much a major factor in criminal justice handling of drug offenses. Incarceration rates by race provide persuasive evidence.

In general, drug enforcement has led the United States to incarcerate more of its citizens than any other country in the world. In 2008, the incarceration rate was just over 1,009 per 100,000 of population, or roughly 1 in a 100. The incarceration rate for European countries, with generally more liberal drug policies, was 150 per 100,000 or nearly seven times lower than the United States.[5] Incarceration rates for the United States, while harsh, take on added significance when racial groups are compared. While drug *use* rates for white and black Americans are roughly equivalent, the incarceration rates reflect significant racial disparity. The incarceration rate for white men in the United States in 2008 was 943 per 100,000 population. For African American men, the rate was 6,667 per 100,000 population. A disturbing comparison is the incarceration rate for black men under the South African apartheid government: 851 per 100,000 populations. The US War on Drugs machine has incarcerated African Americans at nearly eight times the rate of the South African apartheid regime (Cole n.d.).

The sentencing disparity between powder and crack cocaine underlies a portion of the racial gap. In 1986, in the midst of intensive media coverage of the crack cocaine problem, Congress passed the Anti-Drug Abuse Act. The law imposed radically different penalties for sale of crack cocaine versus powder cocaine. Cocaine use patterns between whites and blacks were roughly equivalent, but whites tended to use powder cocaine. Crack cocaine was more used in the black community. The law imposed a mandatory five-year sentence for sale of crack cocaine amounting to five grams. For powder cocaine, it took the sale of 500 grams to reach the mandatory five-year sentence. The discrepancy quickly became known as the 100-1 ratio and its impact was immediately felt. By 2006, over 80 percent of those sentenced under the crack provision were African American.

The harshness of the penalties led even some conservative jurists to protest:

> Judge Lawrence Irving, a Reagan appointee, noted on his retirement, "If I remain on the bench, I have no choice but to follow the law. I just can't, in good conscience, continue to do this." Other judges, such as Judge Jack Weinstein, publically refused to take any more drug cases, describing a "sense of depression about much of the cruelty I've been a party to in connection with the war on drugs." (Alexander 2010, p. 92)

A report by the US Sentencing Commission starkly outlined the outcomes of the Anti-Drug Abuse act of 1986. The study noted that white inmates made up 60 percent of the federal prison population in 1984. By 2004, the percentage of white prisoners had dropped to

35 percent, a decrease driven by an influx of black drug offenders. Looking at drug offenders only, by 2002, 81 percent of all federal drug offenders were black (US Sentencing Commission 2004). The study also found disparity in the length of prison sentences given to white versus black offenders. "While both groups received average sentences of a little over two years in 1984, blacks are now serving an average of six years, while whites are serving only four" (US Sentencing Commission 2004). According to the report, the disparity is partly attributable to the harsh mandatory minimum sentences for drug crimes enacted by Congress.

The 100-1 ratio sentencing disparity for powder and crack cocaine was modified in 2010 when President Obama signed legislation lowering the disparity from 100-1 to 18-1. The order applied only to federal sentencing, and many state laws that had mimicked the original federal legislation remain unchanged.

While the sentencing provision of the 1986 Anti-Drug Abuse Act had a clear racial impact, other racial disparities appear as a result of enforcement practices. A 2013 ACLU study of marijuana arrests found blacks were four times more likely to be arrested on a marijuana offense than were whites. The arrest pattern persists despite the fact that blacks and whites use marijuana at the same rates. The report notes the discriminatory nature of the arrests "creates community mistrust of the police, reduces police-community cooperation, and damages public safety" (ACLU 2013, p. 21). Notably, the report concludes the "War on Marijuana has largely been a war on people of color" (ACLU 2013, p. 9).

The Assault on Constitutional Freedom

Nowhere has the impact of the War on Drugs been more corrosive than its assault on constitutional rights, most notably the right to be free from unreasonable government search and seizure. This right, enshrined in the Fourth Amendment to the Constitution, sets the limit on police ability to stop and search Americans. The amendment reads:

> The right of the people to be secure in their persons, houses, papers, and effects, against unreasonable searches and seizures, shall not be violated, and no Warrants shall issue, but upon probable cause, supported by Oath or affirmation, and particularly describing the place to be searched, and the persons or things to be seized.

The Fourth Amendment was drafted to protect citizens from the arbitrary searches and stops employed by British troops in the colonies.

Within constitutional limits, there are three types of police stops of citizens. The first are "probable cause" stops, clearly falling under the amendment. *Probable cause* means facts and circumstances that would lead a reasonable police officer to believe a crime has been committed and the person stopped committed that crime. Probable cause is the standard for an arrest, or seizure, by a police officer.

A landmark Supreme Court decision in 1968, *Terry v. Ohio* (392 US 1, 88 S. Ct. 1868, 20 L. Ed. 2d 889, 1968), broadened the scope of permissible police stops and seizures of people in circumstances where the officer had neither an arrest warrant nor probable cause for the stop. In the case, a Cleveland police officer had watched three individuals who he believed were casing a store for a robbery. Based on his suspicion, he stopped and searched the individuals, including John Terry, finding guns on two of them. Terry's lawyers claimed the search violated the Fourth Amendment, asking that the gun charge be thrown out because it was the result of an illegal search. A year later, the Supreme Court took up the case.

The Court ruled that although the Fourth Amendment included a zone of personal freedom in which every person is secure from unnecessary and unreasonable governmental intrusion, a police officer may stop and detain a person on observation of conduct that arouses reasonable suspicion of criminal activity. The court ruled the stops should not be unnecessarily restrictive or intrusive and that no search of the individual could be performed unless the officer reasonably believed the individual was armed and dangerous. The *Terry* decision provided the legal basis for police stops stemming from reasonable suspicion.

Terry stops are investigative in nature, and the officer must develop probable cause or the individual is free to go. A Terry stop does not automatically lead to a frisk or search of the individual. The officer must articulate circumstances that lead to his belief the suspect could be armed. Officers can use a variety of reasons to frisk individuals on Terry stops, and the courts have generally deferred to consideration of officer safety as a primary factor. Terry stops have become popularly described as "stop and frisk."

While the *Terry* decision broadened the limits of police stops and searches, a significant portion of police search activity stems from the third type of citizen encounter: a consensual stop. In a consensual stop, a police officer approaches and engages a citizen in conversation but the citizen is free not to answer questions and to walk away (Ohio State Bar Association n.d.).

In *Bostick v. Florida* (89-1717), 501 U.S. 429 (1991) the Supreme Court gave wide latitude to police officers using consensual stops as a wedge leading to searches. Terrance Bostick was on a bus traveling from Miami to Atlanta. The bus made a stop at the station in Fort Lauderdale, and two officers working drug interdiction boarded the bus and woke up Bostick, who was sleeping in the back of the bus. The officers, in green raid jackets and displaying badges and weapons, asked Bostick for his ticket and identification. Bostick complied and the officers told him they were searching for drugs and asked if they could search his bag. Even though Bostick knew he had a pound of cocaine in the bag, he agreed, the drugs were discovered, and he was arrested.

The issue before the Supreme Court was the nature of the encounter between Bostick and the police. If it was truly a consensual encounter, the question before the court was Bostick's ability to refuse the search and leave. The Florida Supreme Court had ruled that because Bostick was blocked from leaving the bus by the officers' presence, it was not a consensual encounter and thus the search was illegal. The Florida Supreme Court decision included an eloquent defense of the Fourth Amendment:

> This is not Hitler's Berlin, or Stalin's Moscow, nor is it the White Supremacist South Africa. Yet in Broward County, Florida, these police officers approach every person on board buses and trains and check identification, tickets, ask to search luggage—all in the name of "voluntary cooperation" with law enforcement. (Alexander 2010, p. 65)

The Florida court had reasoned that an average citizen could hardly refuse a police request when confronted with multiple officers hovering over him, even if the request was phrased as a question. The Supreme Court did not agree, overturning Florida's decision and ruling Bostick's "consensual" search legal.

Other Supreme Court decisions extended the same principle to traffic stops made by the police.[6] The court legitimized the practice of making vehicle stops on minor traffic violations and then seeking permission for a "voluntary" search of the car and/or occupants. Training in the interview skills to secure voluntary permission and the implementation of this tactic by police officers on the street is a mainstay tactic in the drug interdiction stops that occur thousands of times every day across the country.

Another significant area where the War on Drugs has stretched constitutional limits is the use of no-knock search warrants. The "knock and announce" rule related to search warrants stemmed from the belief that "the state is permitted to violate the home's sanctity only under limited circumstances, only as a last resort, and only under conditions that protect the threshold from unnecessary violence." Under this principle, government agents (police) have historically been required by the courts to knock on the door, identify themselves, and provide time for the occupants to voluntarily open the door before they force entry. The courts recognized limited circumstances in which police could force entry without meeting these requirements. These exceptions are known as exigent circumstances and include such factors as a person inside the home in a medical emergency, a violent crime occurring inside the home, an officer in hot pursuit of a felony suspect who entered the home while being chased by the police, and/or a reasonable belief that evidence was being destroyed in the home. Exigent circumstances can allow warrantless searches where an officer has probable cause and no sufficient time to secure a search warrant. Exigent circumstances also allow officers with a warrant to ignore the knock and announce rule and force entry.

Prior to the drug war, the overwhelming majority of search warrants were served by uniformed officers following the knock and announce rules. No-knock warrants were not even in the lexicon of legal authorities until the 1960s, when such warrants were specifically authorized as part of a package of harsh drug enforcement legislation pushed by the governor of New York, Nelson Rockefeller. Thus, no-knock warrants were expanded from a decision a police officer made at the door while serving a warrant to a deliberate tactic for use primarily in drug warrants.

In the years immediately following the legitimation of no-knock warrants, the tactic was seldom used. It was only with the growing popularity of SWAT Teams (Balko 2014, p. 6) combined with the escalating emphasis on drug enforcement that the use of no-knock warrants exploded. Deployment of SWAT teams as part of large city police departments went from 59 percent in 1982 to 89 percent by 1995. In smaller jurisdictions, the percentage of cities deploying SWAT teams went from 13 percent in 1980 to over 50 percent just ten years later (Balko 2014, p. 175).

Originally organized to respond to sniper and hostage situations, the service of drug warrants rapidly became the primary function of

SWAT teams. By 1995, 75 percent of all SWAT deployments were for drug warrants (Balko 2014, p. 75).

The check on the use of forced entry and no-knock warrants has always been the requirement that the judge who approves the warrant closely scrutinize the warrant itself and the necessity for a no-knock entry. But evidence suggests the judicial review of these warrants is more often a "rubber stamp" process than any true check on police power. In a survey of police officers regarding judicial approval of search warrants,[7] journalist Radley Balko found that "most police officers interviewed could not remember having a search warrant turned down" (Balko 2014, p. 75).

With the tactics and weaponry used by SWAT teams, mistakes quickly become tragedies. Raiding the wrong address, bad information from informants, and poor judgment by SWAT leaders and officers has been all too common, and with each incident, police legitimacy takes a hit. Use of SWAT teams in other than dire circumstances, such as hostage or barricaded person situations or a genuine high-risk search warrant, opens the door for not only tragic mistakes but actions calling the competency and professionalism of the police into question.

In 2003, in the small town of Goose Creek, South Carolina, a SWAT team raid on a high school happened after the principal informed the police about a single student suspected of dealing marijuana. Police forced the students to the floor at gunpoint, handcuffing some, and forcibly searching lockers while drug dogs sniffed backpacks. No drugs were found, and no arrests were made. One student's father, a police officer with SWAT experience, said, "They hit that school like it was a crack house. Like they knew there were crack dealers in there with guns" (Balko 2014, p. 85).

Unfortunately, similar incidents have happened across the country with sometimes fatal results. Both civilians and police officers have been killed in ill-conceived and poorly executed raids. The damage done by such police action to community relations and police legitimacy, under the guise of the War on Drugs, is incalculable.

Discussion

The growing movement to legalize marijuana may be only the beginning of a process to wind down the War on Drugs. Ironically, the dire picture of drug abuse in the country may be improving.

Some of the strongest evidence comes from California, which followed its approval of medical marijuana in 1996 by decriminalizing marijuana possession in 2011. A study by the Center on Juvenile and Criminal Justice after decriminalization in California found:

- Teenage crime rates declined.
- Drug overdose deaths (ages fifteen to nineteen) dropped 20 percent, while in the rest of the country it increased 4 percent.
- Marijuana-related DUIs for ages fifteen to nineteen dropped 3 percent, while increasing 12 percent in the rest of the country.
- Violent crime decreased, and drug, property, and other criminal arrests all decreased. (Males and Buchen 2014)

In spite of the often repeated claims that legalization of medical marijuana would lead to increased use of marijuana by teens, evidence does not support that claim. As marijuana laws have liberalized over the past several years, teen use has declined. The Monitoring the Future survey of high school students and the annual National Survey on Drug Use and Health document declining teen use of marijuana. The reasons underlying the decrease are uncertain, but clearly the predicted increase in teen use has not materialized. A summary review of the literature stated, "Findings from dozens of government-commissioned and academic studies published over the past 25 years overwhelmingly affirm that liberalizing marijuana penalties *does not* lead to an increase in marijuana consumption or affect adolescent attitudes toward drug use" (NORML.org n.d.).

While drug overdose deaths have become a leading killer of people in states across the country, a study reported in the *Journal of the American Medical Association* found 25 percent fewer overdose deaths in states where medical marijuana was legalized compared with states without medical marijuana (Bachhuber et al. 2014). The issue requires further study, but it may be that the availability of legal medical marijuana undercuts the illegal heroin and opiate market.

Concern about dramatically increased impaired driving as a result of legal marijuana also appears exaggerated. Fatal crash data from Colorado, one year after marijuana legalization, shows a decline in drug-impaired crashes (Marijuana Policies of Ohio Task Force 2015, p. 22). The concern has always been that marijuana-related crashes would add to the already deadly alcohol-related death toll. But early indicators are that drivers react differently to marijuana intoxication than to alcohol intoxication. One interesting study by the

National Highway Transportation Safety Administration concluded that "alcohol encourages risky driving whereas THC (marijuana) encourages greater caution" (Robbe and O'Hanlon 1999).

Drug law changes in Portugal in the late 1990s offer a starting point for discussion toward an end to the War on Drugs in this country. After struggling with one of the worst drug problems in Europe, Portugal decriminalized personal possession of all drugs, stressed a public health approach to drug abuse, greatly expanded drug treatment capacity, and turned police emphasis from drug users to major traffickers. The Portuguese plan was based on the belief that "criminalization was exacerbating the problem and that only decriminalization could enable an effective government response" (Greenwald 2009, p. 3). The policy changes in Portugal have led to significant improvement in their country's drug problem, particularly compared to the United States, which continues to cling to the criminal justice system as its primary response to drug abuse.

While early drug laws were clearly motivated by racism, more recent drug policies were also rooted in racism of a more subtle nature. The openly racist nature of Henry Anslinger's drug policies, stemming from his disdain for "degenerate races" may be an artifact, but the current War on Drugs also has racist roots.

Early architects of the modern War on Drugs deliberately exploited the racial fears of citizens labeled by Nixon as a "silent majority." The War on Drugs theme was part of the Republican "Southern strategy" designed to lure Southern white voters away from the Democrats. The appeal to Southern whites was consciously based on racial fear-mongering. Presidential advisers H. R. Haldeman and John Erlichman,[9] key Nixon staffers, confirmed the racist underpinnings of the Southern strategy.

Haldeman, White House chief of staff, recalls that Nixon himself deliberately pursued a racial strategy. "He emphasized that you have to face the fact that the whole problem is really the blacks. The key is to devise a system that recognizes this while not appearing to" (Alexander 2010, p. 44). Erlichman, serving as special counsel to Nixon, "explained Nixon's campaign strategy of 1968 in this way: 'We'll go after the racists'" (Alexander 2010, p. 44).

Once Nixon was in office, he was frustrated that his anticrime and drug campaign was faltering. He complained to Haldeman that while the public feared crime, they seemed unaware of anything the Nixon administration was doing about it. Since crime and law enforcement was primarily a local and state function, Nixon's aides looked for some evidence of federal action they could provide to the public. Journalist Jay Epstein noted, "Nixon reminded Erlichman and Krogh there was only one area in which the federal police could produce such results on demand—and that was narcotics" (Balko 2014, p. 103). As a result, G. Gordon Liddy was tasked "to launch an all-out PR offensive to scare the hell out of the public about crime and to tie crime to heroin" (Balko 2014, p. 104).

At the same time, the federal drug enforcement arm, the Bureau of Narcotics and Dangerous Drugs (BNDD), was ordered to shift its focus from high-level traffickers to "making easy, high-profile arrests of low-level offenders that the administration could use for PR purposes" (Balko 2014, p. 103).

Exaggerating the drug problem for political purposes was a strategy continued by successive administrations. Under Reagan, Robert Stuttman, the head of the DEA's New York office, was given the task in 1985 of selling the story of a drug scourge to the US public. In a book published in 1992, Stuttman recalls, "I needed to make it [drugs] a national issue and quickly. I began a lobbying effort and I used the media. The media were only too willing to cooperate" (Alexander 2010, p. 52).

The efforts of Stuttman and others bore fruit. Stories on the "drug scourge," as Stuttman framed it, exploded. Much of the media coverage was on the devastation in the black community as crack cocaine began to sweep through the country. The media coverage was intense, with the *Washington Post* alone running over 1,500 stories on crack in a twelve-month period from October 1988 to October 1989. Alexander writes that Richard Harwood, the *Post*'s ombudsman, "admitted the paper had lost a proper sense of perspective" on the crack problem (Alexander 2010, p. 53).

Crack *was* a serious problem in cities across the country, but the media coverage was sensationalized. The *Los Angeles Times* ran an article in July 1986 that claimed "junior high students are pooling their lunch money to buy cocaine—from schoolyard drug dealers" (Rahtz 2012, p. 85).

"Crack babies" were a central feature of much of the coverage, but subsequent research has debunked much of the crack baby caricature. "Deborah Frank, a Professor of Pediatrics at Boston University, later described the 'crack baby' as a 'grotesque media stereotype.' She found that, in pregnant crack users, the drug's impact on the fetus is similar to the negative effects of tobacco or alcohol use, poor prenatal care or poor nutrition" (Rahtz 2012, p. 85).

Like Anslinger before them, later War on Drug proponents were not shy about falsifying statistics to bolster their political aims, and much of the strategy depended on a well-funded public relations campaign convincing people that the drug problem was out of control. In his book, *The Rise of the Warrior Cop*, Radley Balko provides an example of the statistical shell game played by drug war proponents. The figures relate to the dollar amount of property crime attributable to heroin addicts in 1972.

- Value of the property Nixon claimed was stolen each year by heroin addicts: $2 billion.
- Claimed by South Dakota Senator George McGovern: $4.4 billion.
- Claimed by Nixon drug treatment expert Robert DuPont: $6.3 billion.
- Claimed by Illinois Senator Charles Percy: $10 to $15 billion.
- Claimed by a White House briefing book on drug abuse: $18 billion.
- Total value of all reported stolen property in the United States in 1972: $1.2 billion. (Balko 2014, p. 138)

Ending the War on Drugs would remove a huge impediment to improved relations between the police and the black community. The drug war and resulting mass incarceration has driven a significant wedge between the police and the community. Many of the enforcement tactics have contributed to the mistrust and hostility that underlies far too many police and citizen encounters. Street sweeps, drug market crackdown operations, and the overuse of SWAT teams in drug search warrants have all contributed to widening the schism between police and the community.

Mass incarceration of African Americans may be the clearest manifestation of the harm done by the drug war, but the militarization of police has also been a significant factor. Some police leaders have sounded the alarm in noting how the drug war mentality has "blurred the police mission" (Diane Goldstein 2014). Joseph McNamara, retired chief of the San Jose Police Department, nicely captured the dilemma.

When you're telling cops that they're soldiers in a Drug War, you're destroying the whole concept of the citizen peace officer, a peace officer whose fundamental duty is to protect life and be a community servant. General Colin Powell told us during the

> Persian Gulf War what a soldier's duty is. It's to kill the enemy. And when we allowed our politicians to push cops into a war that they'll never win, they can't win, and let them begin to think of themselves as soldiers, the mentality comes that anything goes. (Diane Goldstein 2014)

Diane Goldstein, a retired California police commander, described the impact of the War on Drugs mentality on a more personal level.

> I also think back with regret to the countless narcotic search warrants that I participated in. After searching for any signs of drugs, we would leave the premises . . . in complete disarray—without worry or concern about the impact on the people who lived there, and without considering the possible harms our actions were causing. (Diane Goldstein 2014)

Winding down the drug war will be a long, difficult, and costly process. The national movement toward marijuana legalization is an important early step in this journey. Despite the liberalization of marijuana policies in the majority of the states, the end of the war on drugs lies much further down the road.

A review of the effort to reform the 100-1 crack sentencing provision illustrates the complexity of the challenge. Although the provision was significantly modified under federal legislation in 2010, that change applied only to federal offenses. The ratio remains enshrined in many state laws passed after the federal legislation in 1986. The federal law was promoted in 1986 as model drug abuse legislation, and adoption of the law by states was rewarded by federal grant largesse.

By numbers, the overwhelming majority of people incarcerated are not in federal prisons but in state jail facilities. In 2013, the total number of state prison inmates was over six times the number of inmates in federal jails (Carson 2013), and even the limited federal effort to undo the 100-1 crack ratio injustice has met legal hurdles.

At issue was whether the 2010 Fair Sentencing Act, which lowered the ratio to 18-1, should be applied retroactively to those convicted prior to 2010. The issue reached the Supreme Court in 2012 (*Dorsey v. United States*, No. 11-5683, 2012), and the court ruled against retroactivity, ordering the new guidelines to apply only to those offenders sentenced after the act's passage in 2010.

The same issue is being faced by states that have legalized marijuana for personal use. Should those individuals serving time on marijuana offenses be released because their behavior leading to the incarceration is now legal? The *Dorsey* decision argues against retroactivity but ignores the racial disparity embedded in the original legislation. The failure of the court to approve retroactivity in *Dorsey* and the presumptive failure of states to approve retroactivity on marijuana offenses only makes permanent the underlying racial bias of the drug war.

The debate on prisoner release is only one part of the dilemma. Should these folks have their records expunged? Should job, housing, and educational assistance be provided to help them on reentry? Community self-interest and a strong commitment to justice argue that a significant effort be undertaken to help these people. Clearing their criminal justice history would be a good first step. For the inevitable protests on the costs of such an effort, it should be noted the expense of modest remedial efforts would likely be more than offset by the savings in prison costs.

Rolling back the erosion of constitutional protections will also be a difficult challenge. Justice William Brennan, one of the greatest civil libertarians to ever sit on the Supreme Court, eloquently articulated the evisceration of the Fourth Amendment by the Court in his dissent in *United States v. Leon*, a decision rendered in 1984. Brennan pointedly noted his court colleagues' willingness to weaken the Fourth Amendment in the service of the War on Drugs. In his dissent, Brennan wrote:

> While the machinery of law enforcement, and indeed the nature of crime itself, have changed dramatically since the Fourth Amendment became part of the Nation's fundamental law in 1791, what the Framers understood then remains true today—that the task of combating crime and convicting the guilty will in every era seem of such critical and pressing concern that we may be lured by the temptations of expediency into forsaking our commitment to protecting individual liberty and privacy. It was for that very reason that the Framers of the Bill of Rights insisted that law enforcement efforts be permanently and unambiguously restricted in order to preserve personal freedoms. (*United States v. Leon*, 468 US 897, No. 82-1771, 1984)

The War on Drugs has led to increasing encroachment on privacy and constitutional rights. Fear of crime and drugs have led people to accept, largely without complaint, the constitutional abuses in drug enforcement. The abuses are shrugged off because they happened to drug users, people viewed as undeserving of sympathy. The good news is that as the failure of the War on Drugs becomes more apparent, elements like asset forfeiture and police militarization are being subjected to increased scrutiny by both citizens and lawmakers.

There are hopeful signs. The New Mexico legislature voted for major reform of the state's asset forfeiture program in 2015. Under the reform, police will still be able to seize assets, but only after proving that a crime had taken place. Furthermore, police agencies are prohibited from keeping any of the proceeds of seized assets, which are now directed to the state's general operating fund. Most notably, the measure passed without any opposition from either party, making it an unusual example of bipartisan cooperation. Governor Susana Martinez signed the bill into law, noting it would "provide further protections to innocent property owners" (Shackford 2015, pp. 9–10).

Some police departments are also changing their drug enforcement strategy. High Point, North Carolina, was one of the first departments to modify their enforcement tactics. Captain Tim Ellenberger, commander of the High Point Major Crimes Division, explained the approach: "Like every other police department, we would do a zero-tolerance sting or a street sweep. While those operations seemed on the face of it productive, they clogged the justice system, felonized people not driving the violence and angered the people who lived there. . . . We weren't making anything better." He added that now "We target the people responsible for the violence surrounding a drug market. It's fairer to the residents. It's smarter policing" (Williams and Herman 2015).

Following voter action to legalize marijuana in 2014, Washington, DC, modified its drug enforcement approach. The emphasis was moved from street enforcement against low-level dealers and addicted customers to a focus on major suppliers. Previously, the DC police made heavy use of "jump-outs" at drug-dealing street locations. The jump-out tactic, used by officers across the country, used plainclothes officers pulling up quickly to a drug location, jumping out of their cars, and detaining all those in the area. Suspects were searched, and some arrests for small amounts of drugs typically were the result. The tactic, though creating a lot of arrests, had virtually zero impact on drug dealing at the location, which quickly resumed as the officers departed. DC Chief Kathy Lanier recognized the price her department was paying with a heavy-handed enforcement effort, and her policy move has drawn praise from police experts and community leaders (Williams and Herman 2015).

Despite some signs of change, the War on Drugs and the racial injustice that has characterized it remain major hurdles to improvement in police relations with the African American community.

Community policing has often been prescribed as the foundation of a positive relationship between police and the community, but the drug war has sabotaged much of that potential. A new effort at community policing that can overcome the hurdles posed by drug enforcement is overdue, and the implementation of such an effort can act as a catalyst for a more peaceful and trusting relationship between the police and those they serve.

Notes

1. Balko's book, *Rise of the Warrior Cop: The Militarization of America's Police* (2014), contains detailed descriptions of multiple SWAT raids on dispensaries, homes, schools, and more.

2. The study on Vietnam vets has been followed by a large volume of research that shows the significant impact of the environment on drug use and addiction.

3. DrugSense.Org, "125th Anniversary of the First U.S.A. Anti-Drug Law: San Francisco's Opium Den Ordinance—Nov. 15, 1875," 2015, http://www.drugsense.org/dpfca/opiumlaw.html.

4. Common Sense for Drug Policy, "The Devil Weed and Harry Anslinger," n.d., http://www.csdp.org/publicservice/anslinger.htm.

5. Jack Cole, "End Prohibition Now," LEAP.cc, Law Enforcement Against Prohibition, n.d., http://www.leap.cc/wp-content/uploads/2011/04/End_Prohibition_Now.pdf.

6. Two notable decisions are *Whren v. United States*, 517 U.S. 806 (1996) and *Ohio v. Robinette*, 519 U.S. 33 (1996).

7. The ease with which search warrants are secured as described by Balko fits my own experience.

7

Repairing the Relationship

The ability of the police to perform their duties is dependent upon public approval of police actions.

—Sir Robert Peel

The communities that need police protection the most, trust police the least. Bridging that divide is the most urgent task for American policing today.

—John Laub

In some communities, the friendly neighborhood beat cop—community guardian—has been replaced with the urban warrior.

—Sue Rahr

National commissions reviewing the riots of the 1960s were blunt regarding the role of police in the disorders. "The police are not merely a 'spark' factor. To some Negroes police have come to symbolize white power, white racism and white repression. . . . The atmosphere of hostility and cynicism is reinforced by a widespread belief among Negroes in the existence of police brutality and in a 'double standard' of justice and protection—one for Negroes and one for whites" (National Advisory Commission on Civil Disorder 1967, p. 9).

Racial attitudes among police officers and patrol tactics came under criticism in the reports. One report observed, "Police lost contact with minority group residents . . . by changing from foot patrols to radio cars, thus removing police from much of the day to day citizen contact foot patrol facilitated" (Sherman, Milton, and Kelly 1973).

The day-to-day contact with community members engendered by foot patrol officers may have been undervalued. In June 2015, former Baltimore Police Sergeant Michael Wood sent out a number of Twitter posts that detailed racist and brutal acts he had witnessed during his time as a Baltimore officer. In an interview with the *Washington Post*, Wood described his "awakening" while doing drug surveillance in the black community. As part of his surveillance, he sat and watched community life for hours on end, gradually recognizing people in the community were not the "enemy" but ordinary folks going about their lives.

> I was doing narcotics work. And so I was spending a lot of time doing surveillance in a van, or in some vacant building. You have a lot of time on your hands with that kind of work. You're watching people for hours at a time. You see them just going about their daily lives. They're getting groceries, running errands, going to work. Suddenly, it started to seem like an entirely different place than what I had seen when I was doing other police work. I grew up in Bel Air, Maryland. I didn't have exposure to inner cities. And when you work in policing, you're inundated early on with the "us vs. them" mentality. It's ingrained in you that this is a war, and if someone isn't wearing a uniform, they're the enemy. It just becomes part of who you are, of how you do your job. And when all you're doing is responding to calls, you're only seeing the people in these neighborhoods when there's conflict. So you start to assume that conflict is all there is. Just bad people doing bad things. (Balko 2015)

While the police were under fire for their role in the riots of the 1960s, research studies documented the ineffectiveness of ingrained police practices. The failure in their most basic mission of controlling crime, together with their role as a catalyst in civil disorder, led to a search for a new approach in policing. Community-oriented policing (COP) promised more effectiveness in addressing crime problems and a new relationship with the community, in particular the African American community. The quality of the police–citizen relationship envisioned in COP echoes to some extent Wood's "awakening."

The path to improved relations between police and African American communities involves two distinct yet related movements. Adoption of COP, a model of policing that relies on community partnerships in identifying and resolving crime and disorder problems, is pillar one.[1] The second pillar is the concept of police legitimacy as the basic framework for all police activity. The community partnerships and problem-solving efforts essential to COP occur in the context of police legitimacy. Without a high degree of legitimacy, the community relationships that foster problem solving cannot develop. Without significant success in problem solving, police legitimacy will inevitably sink under the burden of ineffectiveness. The two are clearly codependent and an effective strategy to close the gap between police and the community must simultaneously address both.

COP

The concept of COP has been stretched over the years to the point that police leaders have included nearly any imaginable police activity as a COP program. Bike patrol, playing basketball with kids, going to neighborhood meetings, and walking the beat in an "Officer Friendly" manner have all been described by police chiefs as community policing (Rahtz 2001, p. 1). James Q. Wilson, who coauthored the "Broken Windows" article that provided the theoretical basis for much of what came to be known as COP, noted, "Community-based policing has now come to mean everything. It's a slogan. It has come to mean so many different things that people who endorse it, such as the Congress of the United States, do not know what they are talking about" (Eggers and O'Leary 1995).

Wilson's dig at Congress aside, his point that broadening COP has left the phrase nearly meaningless rings true. Yet the single theme that has characterized COP is the belief that "increasing the quantity and quality of police-citizen contact reduces crime" (Sherman et al. 1998).

The origins of COP stem from the failure of the primary tenets of modern policing. Random patrol, a staple of police activity, was proven to be ineffective in studies dating to the 1970s (Kelling 1974). Studies likewise found that police rapid response, initiated by the 911 emergency system, was also ineffective, resulting in arrests only about 3 percent of the time (Rahtz 2001, p. 4).

Those findings were buttressed by studies that found policing was largely a repeat business. Research showed over 60 percent of radio runs made to the same 10 percent of addresses; 10 percent of offenders accounting for 55 percent of the crime; and 10 percent of victims involved with 40 percent of total crime (Bieck, Spelman, and Sweeney 1991). Too often, officers treated these repeat runs as individual incidents, one day making an arrest, another day mediating a dispute, another day making a crime report. The underlying reasons repeatedly bringing the police to the situation were rarely addressed. As a result, "police officers begin to feel like hamsters on a treadmill, going to the same locations over and over, seeing the same people and never really accomplishing anything" (Rahtz 2001, p. 11).

In 1982, James Q. Wilson and fellow criminologist George Kelling published their piece "Broken Windows: The Police and Neighborhood Safety" (Kelling and Wilson 1982). This article marked a turning point in the way police officers and managers viewed policing. Wilson and Kelling used broken windows as an analogy for the physical conditions that accompany community crime and disorder. Their contention was that the failure to fix the first broken window becomes a message that the community does not care. In essence, the failure becomes an environmental signal supporting criminal and disorderly behavior. Shortly, all the building's windows will be shattered. The analogy of broken windows included junk autos, abandoned buildings, vacant lots, litter, graffiti, and more.

With Kelling as a consultant, William Bratton, then the chief of the New York Transit Police, decided to test the theory in New York's subways. A common problem in the subways was fare-jumpers—people vaulting the turnstiles rather than paying the fare. Bratton decided to use a crackdown on fare-jumpers as part of a strategy to reduce violent crime in the city's subway system. Fare-jumpers, largely ignored by the police under Bratton's predecessors, were arrested under Bratton's new directive. Drunkenness and other minor violations also resulted in arrest, and in the first four years of Bratton's new policy, misdemeanor arrests increased 500 percent. Violent crime in the subways dropped dramatically and when Bratton later became the chief of the New York Police Department, he extended what became known as "quality of life" enforcement to the city's streets (Gladwell 2000).

The type of police problem solving Bratton implemented also had its origin in research done by Herman Goldstein and outlined in his book, *Problem Oriented Policing* (H. Goldstein 1990). This book identified typical police problems and described a problem-solving approach as a tool to replace the typical reactive nature of police response. Other criminal justice researchers, notably John Eck and

William Spelman, developed a police problem-solving model known as SARA (scanning, analysis, response, and assessment), which was adopted as a tool by police departments across the country.[2] SARA has become a commonly used tool to address the myriad of problems facing the police.

Problem solving is now an embedded strategy in policing. Common police problems and detailed plans to address them are readily available to police officers struggling to solve their beat problems. The Center for Problem Oriented Policing operates a website (http://www.popcenter.org) devoted to police problem solving and provides access to over seventy problem-solving guides on many of the issues facing officers across the country. The guides cover a range of topics, including bicycle thefts, drive-by shootings, ATM robberies, bullying, rave parties, and graffiti. The site also includes guidance on implementing the SARA planning model and interactive learning to assist officers in mastering the problem-solving process.

Many of the difficult and complex problems faced by the police are not so much solved as they are managed. Mental illness among community members is one example. The interaction between people with mental illness and the police is high risk for both parties. By some estimates, as many as a third of the people dying at the hands of the police are mentally ill (Johns 2001). A 2015 examination of deaths at the hands of the police published by the *Washington Post* more or less confirm that estimate. The *Post* reported that of 461 police intervention deaths during the first six months of 2015, 36 percent involved people who had a history of mental illness (Lowery, Kindy, and Alexander 2015).

In a problem solving effort that has been adopted by more than forty departments around the country, the Memphis Police Department developed the Crisis Intervention Team (CIT) Program as an alternative to traditional police response to people with mental illness. The program provided selected beat officers with enhanced training and makes them first responders to any radio runs involving individuals with mental illness. Studies on the impact of CIT-type programs have confirmed positive results (NAMI 2015).

In developing its own version of the CIT program, the Cincinnati Police Department added a twist to the officer training. Each officer selected for the program completed an eight-hour ride-along with a mental health caseworker working in the same neighborhood area as the officer. The ride-along provided the opportunity to meet people struggling with mental illness on the officer's beat—outside of a law enforcement context. It also established a relationship with a mental health professional who could provide support and information for the officer. Although there was some initial grumbling from officers about the ride-along, many later evaluated it as the best part of their training.[3]

Effective problem solving that involves the community facilitates police legitimacy. A program like CIT not only had positive results, but its success served to enhance a view of police as compassionate professionals.

Police Legitimacy

Building and maintaining legitimacy is the biggest challenge confronting today's police leaders. A clear understanding of the concept of legitimacy and how it evolves in the interaction between police officers and community members is key to building a strong bond between police and the community. The strength of that relationship allows for swiftly and effectively defusing tensions when they inevitably occur.

Research over the past twenty years has found people are more likely to obey the law and cooperate with the police when they view the police as legitimate (Mazerolle et al. 2013a, p. 1). Mazerolle and colleagues note efforts to enhance police legitimacy, primarily under the auspices of community policing and problem solving, have demonstrated reductions in crime and disorder as well as reoffending (Mazerolle et al. 2013a, p. 1).

Police action to enhance legitimacy includes departmental action as well as the behavior of individual police officers in every citizen encounter. The style of the contacts between police and citizens is a key factor in developing legitimacy. Sherman and colleagues noted, "One of the most striking recent findings is the extent to which the police themselves create a risk factor for crime simply by using bad manners. Modest but consistent scientific evidence supports the hypothesis that the less respectful police are towards suspects and citizens generally, the less people will comply with the law" (Sherman et al. 1998).

Police tactics to reduce crime also provide an opportunity to enhance or degrade police legitimacy. Problem-solving efforts by the police that damage legitimacy, even if successful, may be a case of winning the battle but losing the war. Commenting on zero tolerance arrests in New York City, Sherman and colleagues found the arrest experience over a minor offense "may permanently lower police legitimacy, both for the arrested person and their social network of family and friends" (Sherman et al. 1998). They further noted an emphasis on mass arrests "may reduce violence in the short run—especially gun violence—they may also increase serious crime in the long run" (Sherman et al. 1998). Police history is replete with examples of crime suppression efforts that antagonize the community. These efforts may even be lauded as successes, but without an appreciation for the long-term costs, the gap between the police and the community will widen.

In the 1980s, the LAPD embarked on a series of operations designed to suppress the drug- and gang-related violence in South Central Los Angeles. Called Operation Hammer, LAPD officers, often numbering in the hundreds, descended on high-crime minority neighborhoods, detaining and arresting large numbers of suspected gang members. The operation reached its peak in April 1988 when over 1,000 officers detained over 1,400 people in a single weekend. The majority of those held were never charged with a crime. LAPD Chief Daryl Gates described the operation as "proactive policing," which he claimed neighborhood residents wanted.

South Central residents did want police protection against the violence. "What the people of South Central did not want was to be treated with contempt and prejudice. Operation Hammer removed hundreds of gang members from the street but also resulted in the rounding up, and sometimes the roughing up, of teenagers whose crime was being in the wrong place at the wrong time" (Cannon, 1999, p.18).

Tactics like Operation Hammer result in the criminalization of large numbers of people caught up in the police net. Even those not arrested for any offense may find themselves entered into a police database of offenders. An investigation of the Denver police database in 1992 found eight of ten African Americans in the city entered on the list of suspected criminals (Pintado-Vertner and Chang 2000, p. 36). Alexander found that a database of the LAPD contained "an overwhelming majority of young black men in the entire city" (Alexander 2010, p. 136).

Police operations designed to suppress crime by sweeps, crackdowns, or high-volume stop-and-frisk tactics run the risk of serious damage to police legitimacy. The choice to implement those tactics must rationally weigh the benefits in crime reduction against the costs in diminished legitimacy. When these operations have a significant impact on African American citizens, the price paid in increased racial tension and risks for disorder need to be part of the community–police discussion that should precede their implementation.

Discussion

COP has been part of police approaches for well over twenty years. Given the continuing tension between the police and the black community, it is fair to say that the promise of COP has yet to be fully realized. Much of the impetus for its implementation was generated by President Bill Clinton's campaign promise of 100,000 officers to be added to the country's police forces and an emphasis on COP as the theme of the additional officers. In a speech outlining his proposal in 1992 (delivered on October 17 in Detroit, Michigan), then-candidate Clinton said, "It is time for America to make a serious commitment to community policing, to having people back on the beat, working the same neighborhoods, making relationships with people in ways that prevent crime."

With his election, Clinton provided federal funding for additional police officers across the country. Funding supported officer training, equipment, and salaries on a gradual phase-out basis, requiring local jurisdictions to take over the costs after the grant period.[4]

In addition to funding for police officers, the COPS (Community Oriented Policing Services) office, established within the Department of Justice to oversee the program, made a significant investment in training police officers—both recruits and in-service officers. With federal funding, a national network of regional community policing institutes (RCPIs) was established across the country, providing free training on COP and problem solving to officers and community members. In 1997 alone, the COPS Office reported training more than 600,000 police and community members on topics including school violence, domestic violence, diversity, and other topics (COPS Office 2015). A major focus of the training was developing collaborative relationships with community partners to solve crime and disorder problems.[5]

The Clinton promise of 100,000 new cops to do community policing never reached that numeric goal. An analysis by the Heritage Foundation (2000) found the program added at most 40,000 new officers to the country's police force. The COPS Office also came under fire for its allocation of the funding. Lawrence Sherman, director of the Fels Center of Government at the University of Pennsylvania, criticized the program for "putting funds where votes are, not where the violence is" (Heritage Foundation 2000).

Some police agencies receiving the funds failed to meet their end of the bargain. Over a four-year period (1993–1997), the Miami-Dade Police Department took $46 million in COPS grants but expanded their ranks by only twenty-one officers. Other agencies actually downsized. Both Atlanta and Washington, DC, police departments took millions in grant funding at the same time they slashed officer positions (Heritage Foundation 2000).

A focus on community policing by the new officers did not fully materialize. Although some departments used the additional officers for community policing, others did not. One of the problems was the lack of guidance provided by the federal government. Balko notes the promise of the additional officers was clothed in Peace Corps–type language, but the implementation in some places accelerated the militarization of the police as part of the drug war. Balko described a funding process for COPS money related to drug arrests. "The size of the disbursements was directly related to the number of city or country drug arrests. Each drug-related arrest brought in . . . $153 to the local department" (Balko 2014, p. 222).

The crime picture in the United States showed significant improvement through the 1990s, and supporters lauded the new police officers involved in COP as the reason for the crime decline. The underlying causes for the crime reduction are complicated and continue to be debated. Theories on the decline include aging of the population, more technology making some types of crime more difficult, incarceration of large numbers of people, and gentrification of inner-city areas previously plagued by high crime rates (Dana Goldstein 2014).

The contribution of the promised 100,000 officers assigned to COP does not appear to be significant. A 2005 study by the Government Accounting Office (GAO) attributed less than 3 percent of the decline to the COPS effort, and a 2007 study concluded "COPS spending had little to no effect on crime" (Balko 2014, p. 222).

The failure of the COPS effort to make a significant and clear contribution to crime reduction is probably more a function of poor implementation than a failure of the concept. The promise of 100,000 new officers made a nice campaign slogan, but nothing close to those numbers was ever deployed. The new officers were supposed to do COP, but lack of accountability measures by the federal government left no adequate records of how many of the new officers actually did so. Balko documents that at least a portion of the COPS funding was used to fund SWAT teams (Balko 2014, p. 221).

The COPS effort was also a victim of circumstances that redirected funding. The bombing of the federal building in Oklahoma City on April 19, 1995, brought the reality of terrorism home to local police departments across the country. Federal funding for police was quickly shifted to equipment and training focused on prevention of and response to terrorist attacks. The 9/11 terrorist attacks six years later accelerated that shift and moved police officers across the country into anti-terrorist task forces and new units focusing on homeland security.

Federal training money followed the shift. Training funds for community policing began to dry up, replaced by programs offering ongoing and extensive training on every aspect of homeland security. Training officers to respond to chemical, biological, or nuclear attacks largely replaced training on community partnerships and problem solving.

The recession in 2008 created significant financial strains on US police departments. For many locales, police hiring was frozen and in some cases, officers faced layoffs. The effect was a dwindling number of officers responding to calls for service. The additional stress on street officers added to the tension embedded in community policing efforts in departments where neighborhood officers, or community liaison officers, attending meetings or working on community projects, were unable to answer radio calls.[6] COPS officers, who worked day shift, were provided offices, and had weekends off, were viewed by some as a luxury. In Baltimore County's Community Policing effort (COPE), "officers were referred to as 'Cops on Pension Early.' In Houston, the Neighborhood Oriented Policing program (NOP) was ridiculed as 'Nobody on Patrol'" (Rahtz 2001, p. 15).

Despite the problems, COP continues to offer a path to improved relations between African Americans and the police. However, unless the program is accompanied and facilitated by an emphasis on police legitimacy, its full potential will remain unrealized. COP and a focus on improving legitimacy together can provide a synergistic effect that could result in improved neighborhood safety and a more trusting relationship with the African American community.

A study in Cincinnati confirms the potential in this dual approach. Eck and Engel, criminal justice researchers with the University of Cincinnati, nicely articulate the postriot changes in Cincinnati policing.

> Specifically in 2002, after a year-long Department of Justice investigation, the City of Cincinnati entered into an agreement to implement numerous reforms within the police department, including changes in use-of-force reporting and training, implementing a risk management system, and creating the Citizens Compliant Authority. In addition, the settlement to a racial profiling lawsuit included the creation of the Cincinnati Community Police Partnering Center, as well as other reforms to improve police-community relations. Years

later, this work continues to flourish as the CPD actively engages in problem-oriented policing as its primary operational strategy and has implemented a variety of strategies to improve effectiveness, transparency, and legitimacy. (Eck and Engel 2015, pp. 8–9)

The results of this effort have been dramatic and include reductions in crime accompanied by indicators of improved community relations. On the crime front, from 2005 through 2014, the city recorded a 44 percent decrease in robberies, a 42 percent decrease in aggravated assaults, and a 41.9 percent reduction in thefts from autos (Eck and Engel 2015, p. 9).

These outcomes were clearly not the result of a heavier law enforcement approach. While crime was declining, Cincinnati officers were making significantly fewer misdemeanor arrests, down 37.5 percent. Felony arrests declined 40.1 percent. Most notably, citizen complains decreased by 42.6 percent, and use of force incidents were down 57 percent (Eck and Engel 2015, p. 9).

Statistics do not fully illuminate the dimensions of the new relationship. An incident in July 2015 illustrates the promise of enhanced police legitimacy when an event with potential to increase tensions between police and the African American community happens.

On July 4, 2015, a crowd estimated at 3,000 was gathered at Fountain Square in downtown Cincinnati for a hip-hop music festival. As the festival ended, some in the crowd threw fireworks at the police detailed as concert security. As officers moved in to arrest those throwing the fireworks, other crowd members assaulted the officers and began to throw bottles at them. Officers called for backup, and as the bottle throwing intensified, police donned riot helmets and moved to disperse the crowd. The disorderly crowd members were largely African American, and in the not-so-distant past, this type of incident would have led to accusations of police overreaction and suspicion that the enforcement and arrests were racially biased.

The reaction of the black community to this incident was mostly indifference. A news interview with an African American woman in the crowd captured the new level of belief in the police. When asked by a reporter for her reaction to the incident and the police response, she said, "We've heard what our police department said, they're on top of it and we have to trust in them and work with each other" (WXIX-TV 2015).

Taking the trust in the police displayed by this woman and multiplying that many times over can provide a foundation to build and maintain a high degree of police legitimacy in the eyes of the African American community. Police departments across the country want to build legitimacy to withstand the incidents and tension that inevitably occur. Building it remains the primary challenge for police leaders.

Notes

1. The term *pillar* is used in the 21st Century Policing Task Force Report to recommend specific steps for police reform. The term is descriptive and I have borrowed it here.

2. I became acquainted with John Eck when he began teaching at the University of Cincinnati in the late 1990s. A slogan he uses in training is "police problem solving is not rocket science. It's more complicated."

3. At the time this training was developed, I was the commander of the Cincinnati Police Academy. The program was put together by a committee of mental health professionals working with academy staff.

4. As a lieutenant assigned to the CPD planning section, I worked on these grants.

5. I was an instructor at the Southwest Ohio Regional Community Policing Institute.

6. COP officers in Cincinnati did not typically respond to radio runs. One day, while doing paperwork in my office, I heard a run request for a wanted subject at a nearby hotel. No cars were available for the run. I grabbed one of my COP officers, and we quickly found and arrested the individual. As we returned to the station with our arrest, we received a sarcastic round of applause from some patrol cops waiting for roll call.

8

Building Police Legitimacy

The reality of policing is that we have not devoted enough time and resources to building relationships with the people with whom we interact the most.

—"Engagement-Based Policing,"
Major Cities Chiefs Association

It changes the relationship when the cop on the beat knows the kid's batting average, doesn't it?

—Fred Carnes, Cincinnati youth baseball coach

The challenge for policing in the United States is stark. Black citizens are much more likely than whites to have encounters with the police, and those encounters are more likely to be viewed as negative. In one Chicago study, nearly 60 percent of black high school students reported having been stopped by the police in the past year, and 40 percent reported that they observed others stopped and treated with disrespect by the police (Flexon, Lurigio, and Greenleaf 2009, p. 185). Criminologist Jamie Flexon notes, "African Americans are more likely than other racial groups to be victims of crime, to have negative contacts with the police, to be stopped disproportionately by the police, and to report incidents of police harassment and mistreatment" (Flexon, Lurigio, and Greenleaf 2009, p. 182).

The frequency of contact between young black men and the police widely exceeds that of police and whites. As one example, a 2006 report found that 70 percent of young black men in Chicago reported being stopped by the police within the past year, compared with an average of 20 percent of the total number of residents in the city (Skogan 2006). The intensity of contact between black men and the police appears to be at least unchanged and likely to have increased over the past ten years. A 2015 poll done by the *New York Times* found that two thirds of all African American men reported being stopped by the police because of their race (Sack and Thee-Brenan 2015). If the poll had focused only on young black men, it may well have exceeded the 70 percent figure from 2006. Although the polls asked somewhat different questions, the size of the gap remains indisputable.

Surveys done over the years illustrate both the depth and the tenacity of the gap between police and African Americans. An NBC News/Marist College poll released in December 2014 found only 12 percent of African Americans expressed a high level of confidence that police treat blacks and whites in an equal fashion. The same poll found trust in the police by African Americans has remained persistently low over the past ten years (Clement 2014). The 2015 *New York Times* poll found "About three-fourths of blacks said they thought that the system was biased against African-Americans, and that the police were more likely to use deadly force against a black person than a white person" (Sack and Thee-Brenan 2015).

The low level of confidence in the police among blacks is even more glaring when compared with white citizens. The NBC News/Marist College poll reported 52 percent of whites have "a great deal of confidence that the police officers in their community treat blacks and whites equally" (Clement 2014).

A 2014 *Washington Post*–ABC News poll found that the distrust of African Americans also extends to the criminal justice system. Poll numbers captured the gaps between the police, the criminal justice system, and the people they serve. On the question of equal treatment for blacks and whites by the criminal justice system, only 10 percent of black Americans thought treatment was equal. When questioned specifically about law enforcement, police fared better with 20 percent of African Americans believing police treat both races equally (Clement 2014).

An interesting finding from the polls is that both black and white people viewed local police more favorably than police in general. Even though a major gap persisted, the finding indicates some potential for local police to positively address the racial gap in their own community (Jones 2015).

The gap between police and black people has not significantly changed over the past twenty years. A 2015 Gallup poll on perceptions of treatment by police found one in four young black men saying they had been unfairly treated by the police within the past thirty days. Dating back to 1997, annual poll results were nearly identical, with only modest changes in both directions. Those small changes are perhaps related to publicity on high-profile events (Jones 2015).

The 2015 Gallup poll found confidence in the police at a twenty-two-year low. Pollsters believe the decline in the confidence rating relates to the highly publicized national incidents in Ferguson and Baltimore. The drop in confidence among African Americans was less stark than that of the general population, generating the somewhat dismaying observation from the report that "One reason blacks' confidence has not changed disproportionately over the last two years is that their confidence in the police was already low, and the recent events appear not to have fundamentally changed their already negative views of the police" (Jones 2015).

The split between black and white is even starker when opinions on recent police force incidents are compared. When questioned on the Ferguson grand jury decision not to indict the officer in the shooting of Michael Brown, 71 percent of blacks said they strongly disagreed with the grand jury compared with only 15 percent of whites who strongly disagreed. Sixty-four percent of whites agreed with the grand jury compared to only 4 percent of African Americans (Fox 2014).

Building Legitimacy

If policing is to close the racial gap, building relationships with the people police are most involved with, African American youth, has to be a priority. A high level of police legitimacy is the foundation of that process.

For the Police Officer

A creative and comprehensive program to improve police legitimacy has the potential to close the racial divide. Legitimacy is built on every action by every officer, and it is created through a deliberative policy framework that recognizes legitimacy as an organizational priority.

As previously noted, researchers found "police themselves create a risk factor for crime simply by using bad manners" (Sherman et al. 1998). But "bad manners," using Sherman's language, can create a much larger risk for a police officer. Police across the country deal repeatedly with the same individuals, and a respectful tone set by those initial contacts can have lasting consequences.

Kalamazoo (Michigan) officer Rick McCall learned the power of a respectful interaction in a heart-stopping moment of a foot pursuit gone bad. Chasing an armed gang member, McCall attempted to vault a chain-link fence. The suspect, who had fallen after his own fence jump, lay on the ground below him. As McCall jumped over the fence, his gun belt got caught up in the fence links, leaving him dangling, helpless, above the suspect. The suspect stood up, took a gun from his waistband, and raised it to McCall. After a terrifying instant, the suspect lowered the gun. "McCall!" he exclaimed, "I didn't know it was you!" (Force Science News 2015). He helped McCall off the fence and allowed himself to be handcuffed without further problems.

McCall had arrested his near-assailant at least three times before. Chatting amiably on one of those occasions, they had discovered they share a birthday, a trivial coincidence the officer used to build rapport and a sense of respect between them. Now walking to McCall's patrol car, the suspect remarked, "Out of all the cops, you've always treated me decent" (Force Science News 2015).

Good police officers have always recognized the importance of treating people with respect.[1] Veteran officers consistently preach the hard-earned wisdom of knowing how to talk to people. The challenge is identifying the specific skills involved, translating those skills into training programs, and follow-up supervision assuring effective street-level performance. There is now research going beyond bad manners and knowing how to talk to people to specific skills for effective communication that builds trust, improves officer safety, and reduces violence.

Mazerolle and colleagues have identified four principles for police–citizen interactions that characterize what is described as "procedurally just behavior." These principles constitute the theoretical base for officer communication to facilitate legitimacy. Those four principles are:

- Treating people with dignity and respect
- Giving individuals "voice" during encounters
- Being neutral and transparent in decision making
- Conveying trustworthy motives. (Mazerolle et al. 2013a, p. 10)

Training police officers to incorporate these principles in their everyday encounters with citizens is the challenge for leadership. There are a number of training programs that focus on providing skills for what is now called engagement policing. The T3 program—standing for tact, tactics, and trust—is one that has been adopted by several departments around the country.[2]

The T3 program has its roots in research conducted by the Department of Defense (DOD). The goal was to better equip soldiers with the social skills to "scout enemy territory, distinguish friends from foes, gather intelligence and resolve conflicts, often with little understanding of the local culture or language" (Schuppe 2014).

Sue Rahr, former Kings County sheriff in Washington State, is a supporter of the T3 program. She notes that war, like police work, is built on individual encounters. "When you're looking at how to build public trust in communities, it's the hundreds of thousands of one-on-one interactions that happen on the street between cops and citizens," she said. Rahr, now leading the Washington State Criminal Justice Training Commission, added, "If those hundreds of thousands of interactions don't go well, you will never build trust." She colorfully notes the solid research base from which the program developed: "This isn't PR or 'hug-a-thug.' This is scientifically based" (Schuppe 2014).

Founders of the T3 program, former police officers who worked in the original DOD project in Iraq and Afghanistan, believe strongly in the potential of the program for US policing. One of the founders, Brian Lande, describes crime-fighting as a social enterprise that turns on individual citizen encounters. Lande believes that with the right tools, those citizen interactions can be shaped. T3 training identifies the skills the best police officers and soldiers use to negotiate even potentially hostile confrontations. He notes, "Officers who can diagnose (or size up) situations well, take time to take the other's perspective, reason about the causes of other's behavior, take time to build rapport, de-escalate conflict, gain voluntary compliance, etc., are able to perform their jobs more safely and are able to keep citizens safe" (Schuppe 2014).

When training police officers, an understanding of the power of legitimacy without the skill set to put it into practice is deficient. An emphasis on the skills involved in a program like T3 takes the concepts of procedural justice from the theoretical to the street. A report on engagement policing for the Major Cities Chiefs Association noted that "social skills must be taught as a core set of proficiencies just like physical training. Social skills should not be taught as a 'topic,' but rather as the foundation of all other policing skills" (Major Cities Chiefs Association et al. 2015).

In addition to the T3 program, there are a number of other communications training programs emphasizing community legitimacy. Among them are Blue Courage, Fair and Impartial Policing, VALOR for Blue, and the Verbal Defense and Influence Training Program, the program adopted by Kalamazoo.

Building police legitimacy in a community is a daily continuous effort consciously engaged in by every member of a police department. Organizational policies and decisions have to align with the goal of building legitimacy. Individual officers will respond to consistency in training, policies, incentives, and supervision, all working to reinforce the desired behavior.

Each police officer, in day-to-day encounters with the public, is the backbone of the effort to build and protect police legitimacy. Police departments, as organizations committed to achieving a high level of legitimacy, also play a major role. Departmental actions—of higher visibility, more widely reported, and affecting all members of the organization—have the potential to significantly enhance or undercut legitimacy.

Organizational Strategy

Brand equity is a concept that corresponds to police legitimacy in many ways. There is little debate in corporate circles about the importance of brand equity. Fatteross notes, "While brand equity is largely intangible, its benefits are anything but" (Fatteross n.d.). The importance of brand equity for corporate success is indisputable, but the stakes for police departments are even more crucial. A brief review of some of the strategy used by corporations to develop and protect brand equity contains lessons for police leaders seeking to strengthen their position in the community.

O'Toole notes that the first step in building brand equity is to identify "the single thing your company stands for to your customers" (O'Toole 2008). For most police agencies, the slogan "protect and serve" would be a simple choice. Yet a review of the poll results listed earlier clearly indicates that for the African American community, the police mission looks very different. O'Toole further notes that the best organizations have "built a special relationship with customers that extends far beyond the product" (O'Toole 2008). With the data previously noted showing African Americans are "more likely to be victims of crime, to have negative contacts with the police, to be stopped disproportionately by the police, and to report incidents of police harassment and mistreatment" (Flexon, Lurigio, and Greenleaf 2009, p. 185), it is clear the police relationship with these "customers" is suffering.

Improving relationships, particularly with African American youth, must be an ongoing and priority process. The President's Task Force on 21st Century Policing recommends, "Law enforcement agencies should engage youth and communities in joint training with law enforcement, citizen academies, ride-alongs, problem solving teams, community action teams, and quality of life teams" (Final Report, p. 46). Creative leaders can expand this list multiple times with efforts directly targeted at increasing legitimacy with this high-priority group of "customers."

In building brand equity, marketing experts emphasize the importance of customer feedback. This is an area also addressed by the President's Task Force, which encourages departments to engage in ongoing efforts to track the level of trust in their community. The report notes police agencies should monitor the trust level in the community just as they measure changes in crime (Final Report, p. 46).

Kalamazoo is a police department that has taken the importance of brand equity to unusual lengths. Following a study revealing African Americans disproportionately receiving traffic citations, Captain Jim Mallery, head of the department's 150-officer patrol force, was determined to change the agency culture. He combined a training effort to improve officer safety and effectiveness in high-risk confrontations with an emphasis on deescalation. In training and in supervision, "Mallery's foundational concept was drilled and re-drilled." He insisted that in *every* contact, "everyone—*everyone*—needs to be treated with dignity and shown respect." He even took the principle to force situations. "Even in a use-of-force situation, after force has been appropriately used there's a definitive moment when the subject deserves to be treated as you'd want a member of your family to be" (Force Science News 2015).

A second prong of the training focused on providing "wow" service to the community. Mallery had a business orientation and designed a program encouraging officers to look for every opportunity to "build the brand" (Force Science News 2015). Kalamazoo officers took it to heart.

Shortly after Mallery's training, an opportunity to build the brand presented itself. Officers were called to the Kalamazoo bus terminal.

The terminal manager was trying to close the building, but twenty people, including small children, who were waiting on a long-delayed connecting bus, refused to leave. Despite the request from the officers to keep the building open, the manager could not be budged and was adamant the closing policy could not be changed. The employee also refused the offer of a police officer staying in the building with the passengers and locking up after the passengers had departed.

With outside temperatures hovering near zero, the officers decided they could not leave the passengers to fend for themselves in the cold. One arranged for a bus from the local transit company to respond and provide a warm space to wait. Another officer, hearing the kids asking for something to eat, went to a nearby McDonald's and bought food for all the waiting passengers.

Two teenage girls, waiting for a connecting bus, tearfully explained they were on their way home to see their dying grandmother. With the girls 100 miles from home and the connecting bus uncertain, officers decided to drive the girls home in a patrol car. When the special treatment was explained to the other passengers, they responded with a standing ovation.

Later, one of the officers involved told Mallery it was one of his proudest moments in a long police career. "That night had an impact on all the officers' hearts," said Mallery. "It was a moment when the nobility of our job touched all the officers" (Force Science News 2015).

Mallery also insists on getting feedback from "customers," including those who are arrested. Twice a month, sergeants randomly phone complainants, victims, and arrestees seeking feedback on officer performance. The feedback is overwhelmingly positive, and the occasional minor complaint is typically dealt with as a "teaching moment" with the involved officer.

The Kalamazoo department is convinced their efforts are showing results. In 2014, the Edison neighborhood was plagued by gangs and gun violence. The killing of a thirteen-year-old during a gang feud and the subsequent conviction of three teens on murder charges helped mobilize the community. Crime declined steeply in 2015, and residents are quick to give credit to the new community emphasis by the police as a major factor in the drop. Tammy Taylor, head of the Edison Neighborhood Residents Association, describes the crime drop as "amazing." Another resident captured the spirit of the new approach by the police, stating, "It isn't always about harassing the youth. They (police) are actually trying to curb violence" (Mueller 2015).

Instilling a culture where everyone is treated with dignity and respect and police officers look for opportunities to provide "wow" service is clearly the base for a program that will positively influence legitimacy. Kalamazoo provides a model for cultural change with an emphasis on individual officer behavior. However, there are some areas where targeted departmental action can realize significant benefits.

Diversity

No discussion of police and the African American community goes on for long before the issue of diversity arises. These discussions occasionally begin with the position that police departments should "look like the community" in terms of ethnicity and gender. Some of the obstacles impeding the recruitment and hiring of a police department that looks like the community have been previously discussed. Police responses to complaints regarding a lack of diversity generally follow the pattern of "We are bound by civil service rules" or "We cannot find qualified candidates." As noted earlier, there may be kernels of truth in both those statements.

What may not be recognized is the potential for building legitimacy that exists in beginning a community-wide discussion on the issue. Instead of being bound by the obstacles of the past, police leaders can enter into a partnership with interested community groups (Urban League, the NAACP, black fraternities and sororities, university African American studies and criminal justice programs) committed to increasing police diversity. If diversity is lacking in the department, a frank acknowledgment of that fact is a good starting point and can be followed with an invitation to work in partnership with police leaders to increase diversity in the department.

The effort by Major League Baseball (MLB) to improve its own diversity provides some lessons here. In 1986, 19 percent of MLB players on opening-day rosters were African American. Over the nearly three decades following, the percentage of black players steadily declined. On opening day in 2014, the number of African American ballplayers on MLB rosters increased for the first time since the 1980s and it appears the steady decline over the past decades has been halted (Nightengale 2015).

MLB recognized that the decline in black players was affecting their bottom line. With the decline in black players, the popularity of baseball among African Americans also faded. In the late 1990s, MLB took action by implementing the Reviving Baseball in the Inner

Cities (RBI) program. From a small program starting in Compton, California, RBI has grown and now operates in more than 200 locations across the country. MLB estimates 200,000 youngsters participated in the RBI program in 2013. Partnering with groups like Boys and Girls Clubs of America, MLB has also funded year-around Baseball Youth Academies in four urban locations that served over 10,000 youngsters in 2014.

Statistics suggest these efforts are bearing fruit. The oldest of the RBI programs in Compton has been particularly effective. Five players coming out of the original program were on 2014 opening day rosters and over thirty others from the Compton program have been drafted by big league clubs (Nightengale 2015).

The number of black MLB players is clearly trending upward. Of the African American players on major league rosters in 2014, 65 percent are thirty years old or younger. Eighteen black players have been first-round draft picks since 2012, and the seven black first-rounders picked in 2013 represented the largest percentage of African American first-round picks since 1992 (Nightengale 2015).

MLB has taken other steps. Their Breakthrough Series, which showcases top minority high school players for scouts and college recruiters, led to sixty players being drafted over the past three years. MLB's Civil Rights Game, begun in 2007 as a spring training game, served as a showcase for the history of African American baseball players, beginning with Jackie Robinson. In 2009, the game was moved to a slot in the regular season, with all players wearing Robinson's number 42, and pregame ceremonies honoring civil rights pioneers.

Lack of diversity in policing is a problem that will only be remedied with a sustained effort. MLB's embrace of inner-city kids at a young age and nurturing some of them into potential professional baseball players contain some elements that could be adapted by police organizations. Of course, only a tiny percentage of those kids who participate in the RBI program will ever play professional baseball. Even so, the program generates an interest in baseball for many of these children and their parents that will result in long-term baseball fandom. The civil rights game and accompanying ceremonies demonstrate a welcoming approach to African American fans.

"Protect the Shield"

While MLB has aggressively approached diversity, the National Football League (NFL) is another professional sports league whose

Protect the Shield program provides a different set of lessons in protecting legitimacy. The NFL aggressively protects its brand with a strong emphasis on respect and responsibility. The unifying theme of the program is "protect the shield," referring to the NFL logo. The privilege of playing in the league and responsibility to team and league are drilled into players beginning at rookie orientation.[3] The image of the NFL is protected by a strong focus on attention to detail, including game-day uniform inspection, control of touchdown celebrations, and more. The program includes a strong emphasis on off-the-field responsible behavior. Players have been sanctioned and fined for behavior and even for comments via Twitter and Facebook that bring negative attention to the league. The NFL also places heavy emphasis on community involvement, working closely with players on charitable events and helping them establish their own philanthropic foundations.

Much of the Protect the Shield program is applicable to policing. It is a privilege to be a police officer, and the job carries a high degree of responsibility. The emphasis on professionalism, characterized by rules governing uniform appearance, has a clear counterpart in police organizations.

Like NFL players, police officers operate in the public eye and their behavior, off the field or off-duty, directly affects the brand. NFL players who use social media in a fashion that embarrasses the league are quickly disciplined. Just as in police organizations, the publicity surrounding inappropriate or racist comments damages the shield. In these instances, police departments, like the NFL, should move quickly to protect their brand.

Social Networking

These days, important announcements or departmental news are more likely to come from Facebook or Twitter than from a traditional press release. A police department's activities on social media can strongly influence community legitimacy. Department websites and Facebook pages should be carefully designed to ensure that the agency's commitment to diversity, transparency, and respect for all are front and center. The agency's commitment to COP and its partnerships with community groups also need to be prominently displayed.

Two of the most important considerations are, first, that social media has largely replaced traditional media for a significant percentage of the population, particularly younger citizens. Second, while traditional media focuses on the negative, there is some evidence that social media outlets will be more likely to focus on positive news.

Bad news sells. Vivek Bapat, a marketing expert, states, "Deeply connected to our emotions, bad or negative news is like a drug that stimulates the senses. It has also sold particularly well" (Bapat 2014). He notes,

> Over the last few decades, television and print outlets have used this knowledge with success. Motivated by their relentless pursuit of attracting more attention (eyeballs) to drive advertising revenue, they act as pushers and carriers of the "bad news drug" and exponentially add to the spiraling, vicious circle. According to some media studies, there are as many as seventeen negative news reports today for every one reporting of good news. (Bapat 2014)

The good news is that much of social media is not driven by the bad news drug described by Bapat. Research documents that people are more likely to share good news than bad news on social media (Bapat 2014). This finding has implications for policing in building legitimacy, and, in marketing terms, "crafting their messaging strategy" (Berger 2014). There is some evidence that the police, operating in the context of protecting the community, can frame their activity in altruistic terms and create strong community support.

A recent survey found that consumers are much more likely to do business with "purpose-driven companies," organizations that "act responsibly and in the best interests of society" (Bapat 2014). Police departments clearly embody what Bapat describes as "aspirational" organizations. Police operate to accomplish the greater good of community safety and thus start with a reservoir of good will. The flip side is that a perceived failure to live up to high community standards results in a degradation of legitimacy, undercutting community support.

The central place of social media in modern life represents organizational risks that can jeopardize effective operations. In Los Angeles in 1992 and Ferguson in 2014, computer messaging and emails sent by police and public officials painted a portrait of organizational racism and brutal policing, eroding the legitimacy of those police departments. The prevalence of Facebook, Twitter, Snapchat, Instagram, and others as part of day-to-day life heightens the potential for serious damage to the police brand by officers using those programs in an unprofessional, reckless, or racist manner. Although a

few will claim that off-duty police officers should have the same freedom of speech as other citizens, the importance of their public role
argues otherwise. Intense scrutiny, both on-duty and off-duty, comes
with the job, and racist jokes over email or other media clearly undercut the ability of the individual and their department to work successfully in the community.

Police organizations must establish a strong prohibition against
any electronic transmissions that could be construed as racist, sexist,
homophobic, or otherwise fosters disrespect for any member of the
community. Some will view this as a concession to political correct-
ness, but in fact the policy provides protection to both individuals and
the organization.

After 9/11, it was clearly understood by nearly all people that
their behavior at airports was now under heavier scrutiny. Airports
have become "no-humor" zones, and the bomb jokes of the past now
receive a rude reaction from security personnel. Although there is
plenty of humor to be found in police work, jokes, cartoons, and
videos that have even a hint of racial animus must be avoided. Even
those items sent or received off-duty, using personal accounts, may
find the light of day in the aftermath of a serious force incident. Any
ill feelings caused by such a policy are in the service of the greater
good in "protecting the badge."

Protecting Legitimacy: Hate Crimes

When a hate crime occurs in a community, it is a significant test of
police legitimacy. Hate crimes are typically defined as criminal
action based on race, religion, national origin, and/or sexual orientation. Local and state ordinances define hate crimes somewhat differently, but in most cases, the "hate crime" designation enhances the
penalty imposed, typically by one level. As an example, an assault,
listed as a misdemeanor one, if designated as a hate crime becomes a
felony five, the next level up.

Some jurisdictions have ethnic intimidation ordinances, which in
essence provide the same sentencing enhancement as hate crime ordinances, but are limited to instances where race is a motivating factor
in the incident.

The additional penalties imposed as part of hate crime or ethnic
intimidation laws represent recognition these crimes have the poten-

tial to undermine the social order. When racially motivated, they increase racial tension and threaten the community fabric. As such, they represent a special challenge to police organizations.

The first priority is the arrest of those responsible. Quick arrests in these incidents act to soften the impact on the community, and the police will rightly be praised for effective investigative work leading to the arrest(s). Imaginative police leaders will use the opportunity presented by these incidents to move beyond a simple arrest to steps to heal the tension caused by the crime. Consider the following two scenarios.

> Scenario One: An African American family moves into a previously all-white neighborhood. Two nights after they move in, the house is vandalized, windows broken, and a message to "get out of the neighborhood" is spray-painted on the exterior walls. The story gets significant attention through traditional and social media, and racial tension begins to smolder. While the search for the suspect(s) is ongoing, the police chief calls a press conference, held in front of the black family's residence. Surrounded by a group of black and white officers, the chief notes the seriousness of the crime, announces the volunteer group of officers with him will be painting over the damage, and invites the neighbors for a get-acquainted cookout that evening hosted by the police department.

> Scenario Two: A white man leaving a college basketball game is jumped and beaten by a group of African American men. Bystanders video the attack and post it on the Internet, and it quickly goes viral. The racial nature of the attack inflames tension, and safety in the area surrounding the campus becomes an issue. The attackers are easily identified via the video and quickly arrested. Recognizing the community tension caused by the incident, the police chief reaches out to the victim, arranging a lunch meeting between them and the university's basketball coach. At the lunch, the coach presents the victim with tickets to the next home game and during the lunch, some of the players stop by, engage in conversation, and exchange a handshake with the man.

In both scenarios, the fictional chief recognized the harm inherent in these incidents. Instead of ending police involvement with an arrest, he took steps to minimize the damage to race relations. The community conversation regarding these events will surely take on a more positive tone as a result of these actions.

Protecting the Legitimacy Balance: When Crises Occur

Police organizations face a particular challenge in protection of their brand. Business organizations typically own a brand unique to their operation. "Police" is a brand shared by thousands of organizations across the country, and a Ferguson-type event becomes a crisis not just for the local police department but in varying degrees an issue for every police department in the country. While the Bank of America certainly faced challenges to its brand during the financial turmoil of the Great Recession, and Shell Oil was similarly challenged by the BP oil spill on the Gulf Coast, their brands were able to rebound as people understood the distinction between an industry-wide crisis and a unique organizational crisis. This distinction is muddied when the police come under scrutiny. Consider a 2015 *Washington Post* headline on a story about police shootings: "Thousands Dead, Few Prosecuted" (Kindy and Kimbriell 2015). Out of the "thousands" noted in the headline, the primary focus of the story was a review of fifty-four questionable police shootings over a ten-year period. The story reviewed details of the shooting incidents and follow-up criminal prosecution, or in some cases, lack of prosecution.

There are more than 18,000 police departments in the country and, as of 2013, an estimated 477,000 police officers working in those departments (Bureau of Justice Statistics 2015). The headline from the *Washington Post*, distributed by Internet sites and media outlets around the world, became an issue for every police department and officer working across the United States. The tenor of the headline and the content of the story ricocheted across the country and fed the perception of the police as brutal, dishonest, uncaring, or racist. There is impact on the brand equity or legitimacy of every police department.[4]

When a police department is confronted with a legitimacy crisis, whether directly related to the actions of one of its officers or "spillover" from an incident elsewhere, effective crisis management can minimize damage to the department. Writing on threats to corporate brand equity, Tybout and Roehm note skillful management of a crisis may "provide opportunities for firms to deepen connections with customers by demonstrating concern and caring" (Tybout and Roehm 2009, p. 84). In dealing with legitimacy threats, speed is essential. The Jack in the Box *E. coli* scandal is a good example.

In 1993, 3 Seattle children died and 400 other people were hospitalized after eating meat contaminated with *E. coli*. On January 15, 1993, Jack Nugent, then president of Jack in the Box, was notified by the Washington State Health Department that an *E. coli* outbreak was "at least partially attributable to hamburgers purchased at Jack in the Box Restaurants" (Department of Defense 2015).

The company waited three days before responding, and then tried to shift the blame. They noted that many of those sickened had eaten at other restaurants as well. Three days after that, they blamed one of their meat suppliers. In a later press release, they castigated the Health Department for failure to notify the company of new standards mandating increased cooking temperatures for the meat.

While Jack in the Box executives eventually moved more deftly to handle the crisis, their stock lost 20 percent of its value, millions were paid out in subsequent civil suits, and their brand equity was severely damaged. It took the company several years to recover. Crisis management experts believe much of the damage could have been avoided with a more immediate response.

For effective brand protection, Tybout and Roehm advise creating a "carefully designed and highly motivated executive crisis-management team" (Tybout and Roehm 2009, p. 84). Team membership should include the "CEO, legal counsel, heads of functions like finance and operations, the firm's top PR person and the VP from the corporate division experiencing the problem" (Tybout and Roehm 2009, p. 84). Having such a team in place is an impossible dream for the majority of US police departments, particularly those outside big cities. Per the Bureau of Justice Statistics, 49 percent of US police departments have fewer than ten officers (Reaves 2011). Smaller departments will be quickly overwhelmed; the situation in Ferguson was an example of events quickly stretching beyond the expertise of part-time administrators and local officials. Nonetheless, the events of 2014 and 2015 should serve as a wake-up call for leaders in communities large and small, and formation of a crisis management team incorporating the best expertise available is an important first step in effectively responding to the variety of incidents, police or otherwise, that may occur.

Brand management experts recommend a four-step crisis response plan. The first step is to assess the incident. For police departments, a situation stemming from action by an officer demands the most immediate attention. The natural reaction of police officials is to view the incident from the perspective of an officer. When the incident involves a police use of deadly force, positions can quickly polarize. It is important to try to understand the point of view of community members and communicate that understanding. When the incident involves a white officer and a black citizen, the situation is complicated by the sometimes ugly history of police and black people. Diversity among the crisis response team will help overcome the mistrust. A preexisting high level of police legitimacy provides the best hope of weathering the crisis.

The second step is to acknowledge the problem. For police leadership, the advice provided for corporate crisis managers could not be more fitting: "Avoid premature statements . . . focus on the process of investigation . . . and prevent further harm" (Tybout and Roehm 2009, p. 84). In no other area does the importance of a complete investigation collide so publicly with demands for immediate action. Time required to complete a thorough investigation may be interpreted as a prelude to a cover-up and demands for action—arrest of the involved officer as an example—may be accompanied by threats of disorder. It is clearly a difficult tightrope for police leaders to walk, and one that might be alleviated by deferring the investigation to an outside agency.[5]

The next step is to formulate a response. A calculation of benefits and costs over the long run provides the accounting for corporate decisions on the crisis response. The formula for police leaders includes not only financial considerations but a cost in lives if the situation degenerates into rioting. The aftermath of rioting historically includes significant economic loss to the community and the likelihood of increased violent crime in the years that follow.

The final step is to implement the response tactics. For police leaders, this means acting with a flexibility that allows rapid change to deal with fluid conditions. Effective management of a crisis has the potential to add to the department's legitimacy account.

Discussion

Building and protecting police legitimacy must be a priority for every police employee, from a clerk at the front desk to the chief. The focus on community engagement reinforces police effectiveness in preventing and solving crime, undercuts the "don't snitch" culture found in many communities, minimizes the racial tension in everyday police encounters, and provides a legitimacy account that will withstand the inevitable police force/shooting incidents that occur.

Establishing a department culture where treating all citizens with dignity and respect provides the foundation for effective policing. Research is clear that effective communications skills by police officers can prevent reoffending and contribute to officer safety. Ensuring dignity and respect as the expected norm during all citizen contacts is a first step in building the department's legitimacy account.

Unfortunately, the legitimacy of every police department is subject to incidents across the country, and a negatively charged event like the death of Freddie Gray in Baltimore reflects on every department and officer. The most important lesson for police leaders is that "Negative news kills brand equity" (Bapat 2014). The fact that the incident occurred elsewhere does not remove the potential for damage to local police legitimacy. Reacting passively to negative news is a strategy that invites the loss of equity. Bapat notes, "With social amplification, bad news happens in an instant—with devastating effect" (Bapat 2014). Every department's legitimacy needs to be aggressively protected, and a crisis plan should be in place to counter the effects of negative incidents. If the bad news is generalized from an incident involving another department, swift and effective use of social media can help minimize the impact.

Social media also provides an opportunity to react to developing problems quickly. Tybout and Roehm note, "Savvy companies today not only monitor the web and social media for budding scandal but also use these platforms to acknowledge customers' concerns and keep people informed" (Tybout and Roehm 2009, p. 84).

If the incident involves your organization, the crisis demands an immediate response. The advice for business organizations facing a brand equity crisis is applicable. "The best way to counter is to act immediately and decisively before the bad news spreads. Own up to your mistakes. Fix problems. Be sincere and upfront. Respond personally and responsibly to complaints. Get your leaders in front of the news" (Bapat 2014).

Responding to potential problems is only half the equation. Building brand equity must be a priority. As part of their effort, some departments believe in seeking those wow! moments in providing police service. In every department, opportunities abound for police officers to make contributions to the legitimacy account. An act of kindness by a Louisville police lieutenant illustrates this point.

Asa Ford, an African American woman, was inspired to lose weight after her husband lost a limb to diabetes. After losing more than 200 pounds, Ford signed up for a 10K race in her home city of Louisville.

The day of the race, she made it through the first five miles, but then began struggling. Lieutenant Aubrey Gregory was staffing a traffic post at the five-mile mark and noticed Ford, in tears and struggling to catch her breath. Ford was determined to finish the race, and after checking her well-being, Gregory took her arm and walked her to the finish line. The photo of Ford, arm in arm with the white uniformed officer, got national attention, with effusive praise for both Ford and Gregory. Ford's son Terrance spoke for a lot of people when he said, "With all the stuff that's going on with police it's nice to know there are good people out there" (Lacey-Bordeaux 2015). Lieutenant Gregory's simple act of compassion paid dividends in legitimacy not only for the Louisville PD but for police officers and departments across the country.

Opportunities to build legitimacy are not limited to acts of kindness. The courage displayed by police in life-threatening events adds to legitimacy. In Chattanooga, a man named Mohammad Youssuf Abdulazeez, armed with an assault rifle, a shotgun, and a 9mm handgun, launched an attack on two military recruiting stations, killing four marines and a navy officer. Chattanooga officers rushed to the gunfire, engaging Abdulazeez in an intense firefight, where he was able to wound one officer before being killed. Chattanooga Chief Fred Fletcher rightfully praised his officers, calling the incident a "breathtaking example of everyday courage" (McClam and Williams 2015).

Thousands of times every day, police officers act with courage and compassion, and only on occasion do these incidents receive widespread attention. Police leaders, understanding the power of legitimacy, will view these acts as opportunities to make deposits into their legitimacy account. The key is simply to acknowledge what occurred and then use social and traditional media to spread the word.

An officer coaches a youth football team—a Facebook post with a picture of the officer along with some team members and parents shouts community engagement. A new African American officer is hired. An interview on the department's web page displays agency commitment to diversity. Officers apprehend a rapist. Effectiveness in solving crime adds to the legitimacy account. The department partners with black churches to create a youth police academy. Pictures on Instagram and Facebook posts can create a ripple of goodwill among a group where mistrust of the police is endemic.

There is no need to manufacture events or dust off the old-style PR campaign. The challenge is to recognize opportunities and make use of them effectively with a particular emphasis on social media.

These efforts provide no guarantee. The department's legitimacy will be challenged, particularly as incidents intersecting police use of force and race occur. Community engagement should directly address the use-of-force issue through an open and comprehensive discussion including a wide swath of the community. The current focus on the troubled relationship between police and African Americans represents an opportunity for forward-thinking police leaders, and community forums are one tactic that can effectively begin the conversation.

Notes

1. I have heard similar stories from other officers.
2. See http://www.polis-solutions.net/#!t3/c1v4j.
3. A rookie camp speech by former NFL head coach and football analyst Herm Edwards can be found at https://www.youtube.com/watch?v=ux3GFoNIW3o.
4. The story was accurate, but context was lacking.
5. Postforce investigations are dealt with more fully in Chapter 10.

9

Stopping Riots Before They Start

We recommend that the police and militia work out, at the earliest possible date, a detailed plan for joint action in the control of race riots.

— Chicago Commission on Race Relations (1922)

Law enforcement agencies should schedule regular forums and meetings where all community members can interact with police and help influence programs and policy.

— President's Task Force on 21st-Century Policing

We need to talk about these things in order for them to change.

— Dave Chappelle, comedian

There is increasing recognition that the rift between police and the African American community in the United States needs to be directly addressed. A variety of efforts are under way. Russell Simmons, co-founder of Def Jam Recordings, is funding programs in Chicago, New Orleans, Cincinnati, and Los Angeles. The programs bring police and local teens together in basketball leagues. Simmons, who has a long history of involvement in projects to better the community, noted that relations between police and residents are key to reducing violence. In a statement announcing the grants, he nicely captured the essence of police legitimacy. "We have to respect law enforcement. We have to have police respect the community" (Tweh 2015). Simmons also supports a number of other initiatives, including body cameras for police, state investigations of fatal police shootings, and an end to the drug war.

While high-profile leaders like Simmons are pushing for change, ordinary citizens are also mobilizing. Reginald England owns the Hair on the Floor barber shop in Covington, Kentucky, and heard a lot of concern from the community on relations with the police. England, who grew up without parents and served time in prison, organized a flag football league with local police and firefighters playing with neighborhood kids. "My whole goal is to bring the community and cops in together," he said. "For kids that don't have guidance, have them come to this program and find the right path" (Wartman 2015).

The efforts of people like Simmons and England demonstrate a level of community concern that can lead to a direct effort at closing the racial gap. Issues for closing the gap between police and the African American community include engagement, transparency, legitimacy, and partnerships in solving problems. The development and maintenance of these elements requires ongoing and long-term attention. The aftermath of events like the unrest in Ferguson and Baltimore, together with the high level of community concern, provide an opportunity to jump-start this effort.

Combining these ingredients in a community outreach effort with the goal of riot prevention provides a litmus test of police willingness to partner with their community. It is also an opportunity for African American citizens to share their vision of what policing should look like. Most important, the process represents a leap forward in closing the gap between the police and black citizens.

The proposed process is best described as a forum discussion on police and community relations. The actual title is a decision for planners, and there are multiple options. The title might be generic: "A New Beginning: Police and the Community" would be one example. Or the title might be more specific: "A Community Discussion on Police and Race." While riot prevention is the main goal, some police and political leaders will shrink from such a blunt description. Few community leaders are willing to admit that the potential for civil disorder exists in their area. In addition, there is a segment of the public who believe that even acknowledging the possibility somehow invites disorder. Regardless of what you call them, riot-related issues need to be clearly and forthrightly addressed.

Getting Started

The first step is a commitment by political and police leaders to declare themselves open to community input. Once the commitment to a public discussion of police and community issues is made, the logistics of the program take precedence. Who will attend, how many, length of the program, food and drinks, media participation, group leaders, and so on—all need to be considered. Some of the nitty-gritty details can be handled by an event planner, but the outreach effort to the community needs to be carefully done.

Planning for a forum discussion offers the opportunity to build lasting partnerships. Cosponsors should include local chapters of groups such as the Urban League and the NAACP. Black Lives Matter has become a national group, and their organization could be involved where they have a local presence. Local universities can be invited to provide facilities and meeting space as well as providing staffing and assistance in training of group leaders.

Participants should reflect the community. With that as a baseline, the inclusion of African Americans, particularly youth, needs to be a priority. Student leaders from local high schools would be a natural addition. Outreach to black churches and invitations to ministers and youth leaders would add to youth involvement. A targeted invitation to a minister including invitations for two youth members of the church might be an effective approach. Many universities have African American studies departments, and students in these programs as well as criminal justice students might be willing to volunteer to assist as group leaders.

Only space and time constraints should limit the number of participants. If interest in the forum exceeds the logistical ability of the setup, the event can be repeated. The depth of community involvement is crucial, and planning efforts need to ensure the widest possible involvement of African American citizens, particularly youth.

Forum Leadership and Structure

The suggested format for a forum includes general presentations and small group work. A brief initial welcome address by the mayor and/or city manager will demonstrate official support. Presentations to the whole group should cover topics that reflect community concern, with an emphasis on use of force as well as prevention of and response to civil disorder. A brief presentation on riot history with an emphasis on lessons learned would lead to discussion on a number of more specific issues. What are the procedures for policing lawful protest events? How can the community and police work together to prevent peaceful protests from escalating into disorder? If disorder occurs, what plans are in place for responding? How should police respond? Can a joint police–community response team be effectively utilized? If disorder spreads, at what point should additional resources, like the National Guard, be deployed? What is the process for requesting state and/or federal assistance, and what resources do these organizations bring to establishing peace? How will neighborhood businesses be protected from looting? What should be the police response to looting?

The issue of racial bias in policing needs to be forthrightly addressed. Acknowledgment of the sometimes ugly history of police in the African American community is a good starting point with an emphasis on learning from the past, not dwelling in it. Moving forward is the theme.

Police use of force would be a major focus of the forum. Specific issues might include department policy review, force options provided to officers, the investigation process when force incidents occur, training officers for use of force, and disciplinary steps for those involved in excessive force incidents.

There are a number of other topics worth including. Police and community problem solving, hiring procedures and department diversity, use of in-car or body cameras, and even uniform choices might be addressed.

Forum Staffing

The staffing of the forum event should reflect the diversity of the community and the shared responsibility for public safety. Small group sessions, which constitute the bulk of the event, can be co-led by a police officer and a community representative. Community staffers can be recruited through local churches, interested organizations, and universities. Maturity, good communications skills, commitment to the community, and openness to new ideas are among the qualities required.

The selection of police officers to co-lead small groups will also reflect the characteristics listed above. The take-charge style of some officers, appropriate in certain street situations, will be counterproductive in a community discussion setting. A training session for all staffers will allow for the development of a relaxed and comfortable relationship between police and citizen group leaders. Training for forum leaders should emphasize small group leadership and group dynamics.

The Forum Product

Recommendations for changes in policy and procedures are a certain outcome of the forum discussion. The commitment by police leaders to implement such recommendations represents a level of trust in the community that will positively influence legitimacy.

Proceedings should be recorded and made easily available online. As recommendations are discussed, implemented, or discarded, updates should be posted.

The commitment to transparency made at the opening of the forum will be tested. The written record provides a benchmark for true community engagement, and police and political leaders should remind participants and media of their responsibility to hold officials accountable for implementation. The failure of a police department to implement reasonable recommendations coming from forum participants will represent a backward step and damage the legitimacy established.

A concrete report of conference proceedings will be the most visible product of the forum, but it will not be the most important outcome. If done well, the outcome will be an increase in trust as participants establish working relationships with police officers, see their input taken seriously, and become involved in a long-term program to make their community a safer place for all residents.

The potential for change can be seen in the Cincinnati experience. After the 2001 riots, under pressure from the Department of Justice, the city, the ACLU, Black United Front, and the Fraternal Order of Police all signed on to what became known as the Collaborative Agreement.[1] The overriding theme of the agreement was a commitment to what was labeled community problem-oriented policing (CPOP). The essence of the CPOP provision was a promise by the police department to make CPOP the driving philosophy of the department.

The agreement also mandated some specific policy changes agreed on by the parties.[2] These included the establishment of a new, independent Citizen Complaint Review Board, a new pursuit policy, mental health training, and changes in policy and training for use of force. Perhaps the most important new program was the establishment of the Community Police Partnering Center, providing structure and support for citizen involvement in problem-solving efforts.

Many of the department's command staff were resistant. Assistant Police Chief Paul Humphries noted, "Some had to be drug along with their heels dug in the sand, but we made a lot of changes and we're better for it" (Bronson 2014).

The Collaborative Agreement marked a turning point in police relations with the African American community in Cincinnati. From the low point of rioting and an economic boycott in 2001, subsequent changes in the city included election of a black mayor, appointment of a black police chief, and substantial police outreach to the community as a result of the Collaborative Agreement. In 2008 the city welcomed the national NAACP Convention. The city and particularly its police officers made a determined effort to welcome all the convention attendees. On the final morning of the convention, during his breakfast address, Cincinnati Mayor Mark Mallory thanked the various groups that had worked to make the convention a success. When Mallory mentioned the Police Department, the delegates stood and cheered. Mallory said, "The crowd just went crazy. It was beautiful" (Prendergrast 2008).

The new relationship between the police and African Americans has continued to thrive over the ensuing years. In 2015, US Attorney General Loretta Lynch described the collaborative model in Cincinnati as one other cities should follow. "Everyone has to decide at some point that we're going to sit down and . . . after we've all talked at each other, we're going to talk to each other," she said. "Cincinnati has been able to do that" (Grasha 2015). Statistics support the collaborative model claims. From 1999 to 2015, police force incidents declined nearly 70 percent and resident complaints dropped 42 percent (Hunt 2015).

Discussion

There is no shortage of ideas for bridging the gap between police and African Americans. Norm Stamper, the former chief of police in Seattle, believes the first step is the formation of a "large, representative, credible crisis team to work with the police, communicate systematically with the community and, most importantly, elicit grassroots suggestions for resolution of the conflict. While some leaders have already tried to do this on an *ad hoc* basis, their work needs to be institutionalized and expanded to include others" (Stamper 2014). Stamper would also open up police performance issues for community input. He calls for the formation of a "group of citizens, officers, politicians and civic leaders to craft and quickly implement a statement of non-negotiable standards for the performance and conduct of each and every police officer (Stamper 2014).

Ed Rendell, former mayor of Philadelphia and governor of Pennsylvania, also would use citizen input. "I'd form an advisory committee on community relations, with people of all colors. They'd meet every two weeks, have an agenda, hear any gripes. And the mayor has to sit there throughout every meeting" (Hampson, Bello, and Johnson 2015).

Stephanie Rawlings-Blake, the mayor of Baltimore, says of the police and the community, "Everyone has to face the fact they're in a relationship. It can be a good relationship or a bad one, but they're married. They have to figure out what kind of a [relationship they want] to have" (Hampson, Bello, and Johnson 2015).

Suggestions have also been made by families of those who died at the hands of the police. Wanda Johnson, the mother of Oscar Grant, killed by a police officer in Oakland in 2009, formed a foundation to fight police brutality. She believes police officers need a deeper connection in the community. One suggestion: "Have all officers, wearing civilian clothes, perform community service in the neighborhoods they patrol—fundraisers, social events, whatever helps them get to know the people they're supposed to protect" (Hampson, Bello, and Johnson 2015).

The aunt of a man killed in an accidental shooting by a police officer in New York supports the idea of a community conversation. Hertencia Petersen believes the only way for community–police relations to improve is if "people sit down and air things out" (Hampson, Bello, and Johnson 2015). She supports the idea of community forums with everything up for discussion. "We have to listen to each other, even if we agree to disagree. So far, it's all been, 'My way or no way'" (Hampson, Bello, and Johnson 2015).

There is widespread agreement that improving relations between police and the African American community is the path toward community peace. A particular focus on the relationship between young people and the police is an element supported by nearly everyone. Athletics, like the flag football league proposed by a Kentucky barber, or basketball, as supported by Russell Simmons, is viewed as a natural connection.

The idea of a community forum builds on the foundation of increased communication and adds specificity and structure to the conversation. A police department opening up its operations to input from the black community enhances the potential for long-term change. The expectation is that agreed changes or consensus on police operations will strengthen relations with the African American community. The more important outcome will be a significant contribution to police legitimacy. The content of the forum will be secondary to the group process that occurs.

The collaborative model in Cincinnati provides some positive history. In the aftermath of a riot, and forced together by the threat of federal intervention, the atmosphere in the early stages of discussion was tense. At one of the early group sessions, police in the room clustered on one side and community representatives gathered on the other. It closely resembled a junior high dance with boys and girls gathered in their own groups.

Don Hardin, a long-serving Fraternal Order of Police attorney and ardent supporter of the police, stood and announced the purpose of the gathering was to get to know each other. He seated himself next to the Black United Front representative. Hardin's action broke the ice and set the stage for the groups to begin to work with one another.

Peter Bronson was a columnist working for the *Cincinnati Enquirer* during the years prior to the 2001 riot and for a few years after. He was a witness to the change that has happened since 2001. In a guest editorial for the *Wall Street Journal* on steps Ferguson might take in the aftermath of the 2014 rioting, Bronson referred to his Cincinnati experience. "Before the riots there was simmering anger at police in the black community. The police were insular and authoritarian. Today they are proactive, transparent, a model of community-oriented policing" (Bronson 2014).

There is nothing magical about the recommendation for a community forum. Working in groups is how humans have approached problems since the beginning of time. The key element here is the decision by police leaders to open up their department to true community engagement. The process that occurs will bring to fruition the wisdom of Sir Robert Peel's principle: The police are the public and the public are the police.

Organizing a community forum can be easily accomplished, but the forum has to be the first step in a larger effort. Maintaining police legitimacy is a long-term and continuous process. Jump-starting this process through a forum-type event begins with the invitation to the

African American community to become real stakeholders in the policing of their community. The goal is to develop a level of trust bridging the gap between police and the community. Effectively done, results include increased cooperation in solving crime problems, ending the "don't snitch" culture embedded in mistrust of the police, and providing a legitimacy strong enough to immunize the community against the tension and disorder following a police force event.

Notes

1. See http://www.cincinnati-oh.gov/police/department-references/collaborative-agreement/.

2. I was the commander of the Cincinnati Police Academy and was heavily involved in collaborative-driven changes in training.

10

Moving from Ideas to Action

Reason is the solution. It is mightier than the six-shooter.

—Chicago Commission Report, 1919

I read that report . . . of the 1919 riot in Chicago, and it is as if I were reading the report of the investigating committee on the Harlem riot of '43, the report of the McCone Commission on the Watts [1965] riot. I must again in candor say to you members of this Commission—it is a kind of Alice in Wonderland—with the same moving picture re-shown over and over again, the same analysis, the same recommendations, and the same inaction.

—Kenneth B. Clark, testimony to the Kerner Commission, 1967

By constitutional design, policing in the United States is the responsibility of state and local government. Over 18,000 separate police departments provide the mosaic of police service. Ultimately, closing the gap between the black community and law enforcement will require the work of thousands of police organizations successfully reaching out and truly engaging the citizens they serve. Action by state and federal authorities will facilitate the process.

Oversight of police organizations has largely been left to local jurisdictions. Events of the past few years highlight areas where increasing state oversight of local police would be not only appropri-

147

ate but constructive. Nearly every state provides a minimal level of oversight, primarily through the police officer certification process. States typically have a bureaucratic entity, a commission on Police Officer Standards and Training (POST), which sets minimal requirements for employment as a police officer and mandates completion of a state-approved training program (Police Academy). Certification by the state is a prerequisite for employment as an officer.

There are four specific areas where state-level organizations can provide appropriate regulatory authority, enhancing the professionalism and effectiveness of US policing. The first is the use of decertification power as a check on excessive use of force and other officer misconduct.

State Oversight on Misconduct and Excessive Force

State police commissions could be tasked with regulatory overview of officer discipline in serious force and misconduct cases. While state commissions possess the authority to decertify police officers, this authority is not often utilized. These bodies could be empowered to act much in the manner of state medical boards or state bar associations. Those bodies investigate complaints and act to disbar unfit lawyers or revoke the license of unfit doctors. A state police commission could assume this same role. The case for a strong state body providing oversight on police misconduct is compelling. "No state assumes that the public interest is adequately protected by leaving the ultimate discipline of lawyers and doctors up to law firms and hospitals. Similarly, given the costs to our society of unfit police officers, the final decision of whether or not a person remains in law enforcement cannot be left up to local departments" (Goldman and Puro 2001).

Even in cases of fatal police shootings, these commissions could play a significant role. The current procedure following a police shooting uses the criminal justice system—a necessary process, but one ill-equipped for most cases. The majority of police shootings are legally justified, and the courts have rightly ruled that officers must be given the benefit of the doubt in circumstances, as noted by the Supreme Court in *Graham v. Connor* (490 U.S. 386, 1989), that are "tense, uncertain and fast evolving."

Only a very small percentage of police intervention deaths result in criminal charges. A study by Bowling Green University researchers covering the past decade found fifty-four officers charged in fatal police shootings, a fraction of the thousands of police shooting deaths over that period (Kindy and Kimbriell 2015). Those cases where charges were filed usually had a number of unusual circumstances, including video of the incident, incriminating testimony from other officers, and/or indications of a cover-up. Even where officers were charged, convictions are unlikely; when convictions occur, jail sentences, if imposed, tend to be minimal (Kindy and Kimbriell 2015).

Philip Stinson, one of the authors of the Bowling Green study, noted, "To charge an officer in a fatal shooting, it takes something so egregious, so over the top that it cannot be explained in any rational way. It also has to be a case that prosecutors are willing to hang their reputation on" (Kindy and Kimbriell 2015).

Some police critics have interpreted the low number of criminal charges and convictions in police shootings as evidence of cover-ups in police force incidents. In fact, there are two reasons for the low number. The first is that the overwhelming majority of these shootings are legally justified. The *Washington Post* review of all 2015 police shootings found "In three-quarters of the fatal shootings, Police were under attack or defending someone who was" (Kindy et al. 2015). The second reason underlying the low percentage of charges and subsequent lack of convictions is rooted at least partly in the fact that "the criminal law and its sanctions are a blunt instrument largely unsuited for judging the complexity of force incidents. The law itself provides officers with tremendous latitude in force situations, asking only that the officer act in a 'reasonable' manner" (Rahtz 2003). Furthermore, juries are reluctant to impose criminal guilt on an officer "just doing his job." Cheh notes, "Jurors are naturally sympathetic toward an officer, who, after all, became involved in the incident as part of his duties. They are reluctant to brand him a criminal and find beyond a reasonable doubt that he committed a crime. Contrariwise they usually see the victim as unsympathetic, as contributing to the event, or as a criminal who deserved what he got" (Cheh 1995, p. 243).

This recommendation does not preclude criminal charges. If the investigatory body responsible decides that criminal charges are appropriate, any action by state commissions would be deferred. When the criminal justice process is complete, the commission could review these incidents outside the context of criminal action and without the necessity for proof beyond a reasonable doubt. In the same fashion as medical boards and bar associations, police commissions could decertify an officer, effectively ending his police career. In fact, forty-three of the state certification bodies have the explicit authority to revoke officer certifications (Goldman and Puro 2001). This action by a commission would fall in an area where criminal guilt was not established but a variety of other factors may come into play.

State commissions have revoked the certification of officers following substantiated complaints of misconduct. In St. Louis, an officer discovering marijuana in a woman's car offered to drop charges if she agreed to have sex with him.[1] The woman agreed to the sex but subsequently reported the incident. The officer's certificate was revoked by Missouri in 1999 (Goldman and Puro 2001).

In another case, an officer who perjured himself in court was charged with a misdemeanor and subsequently decertified by Missouri authorities. The number of certificate revocations are small, but a 2001 study in St. Louis found the numbers increasing and noted officers in the prior years had been decertified for "sex with arrestees or inmates, theft . . . assault and positive drug tests" (Goldman and Puro 2001).

The case for stronger and more frequent use of the revocation authority is nicely articulated by the authors of the 2001 study.

> Traditional remedies for police misconduct fail to address the problem caused by the practice of leaving the decision to hire and fire officers up to local sheriffs and chiefs. This often leads to situations where unfit officers are able to continue to work for a department that is unable or unwilling to terminate them. Even when they are terminated, these officers often go to work for other departments within the state. Although virtually every other profession is regulated by a state board with the power to remove or suspend the licenses or certificates of unfit members of the profession (e.g., attorneys, physicians, teachers), there has been a longstanding tradition of local control of police without state involvement. (Goldman and Puro 2001)

The notable failure of local authorities to discipline or terminate problem officers strengthens the case for state revocation action. A state body could have its own investigative staff that would process complaints in the same manner as grievances filed against lawyers and doctors. The commission could defer to local authorities or conduct their own investigation and impose discipline, even where the local police department does not. Evidence from across the country suggests that police departments are notoriously unable to terminate problem officers, even in circumstances when doing so would appear to be a clear choice. There are a multitude of examples.

Oakland Officer Robert Roche was policing a 2011 Occupy protest. One of the protesters, Iraq War veteran Scott Olsen, was hit in the head with a bean bag round and collapsed with a fractured skull. As other protestors gathered around Olsen, Roche threw a flash grenade into the group. He was fired after an internal investigation substantiated a complaint of excessive force. Roche was later reinstated by an arbitrator (Friedersdorf 2014).

In another case, an internal investigation by the Sarasota Police found that Officer Scott Patrick punched and choked a man while arresting him at a local nightclub. The incident was caught on video, and evidence forwarded to the local prosecutor, who declined to press charges. Per the Sarasota Police Chief, "First, he punched an individual an excessive number of times. Second, he had an opportunity to stop after the person's arm was pinned but failed to do so. Third, he made a statement immediately after the incident that 'I should have killed him.'" Scott was fired, but was put back on the job by an arbitrator who lowered his punishment to a thirty-day suspension (Friedersdorf 2014).

Police officers accused of sexual misconduct have also benefited from arbitration. Lakeland (Florida) Police Sergeant David Woolverton was fired after his chief testified he has "a history of sexual misconduct or allegations of this behavior that goes back a number of years" (Friedersdorf 2014). Woolverton admitted to having sex with a colleague in a city park, but denied that colleague's accusation he had forced her to have sex on her desk at police headquarters. Woolverton had been disciplined earlier in his career for an inappropriate relationship involving a high school student who was interning with the department. In view of his record, "State Attorney Jerry Hill notified the department she would no longer accept his testimony in criminal cases" (Friedersdorf 2014). Woolverton appealed his firing, and an arbitrator overturned his termination, reinstating him and awarding him a year's back pay (Friedersdorf 2014).

Unfortunately, these cases are not rare exceptions. The hundreds of similar ones reported across the country create a public perception that officer misconduct is routinely covered up and tolerated. The failure of local police to impose reasonable discipline strongly supports increased state oversight. In the Oakland case of Roche, "Federal Judge

Thelton Henderson ordered an investigation of the Oakland Police Department's disciplinary appeals process, writing that 'imposition of discipline is meaningless if it is not final'" (Friedersdorf 2014).

With the authority to decertify police officers and following the model of state bar associations and medical boards, state police commissions would provide a significant safeguard against the continued employment of abusive and criminal police officers.

In addition to revocation authority, state commissions could take action independent of the employing agency, including ordering discipline short of decertification. Again, similar to the action of medical boards and bar associations, officers could be put on probation, have their certification suspended for a period of time, be ordered to retraining, or a variety of other remedial steps. The threat of decertification would be the hammer reinforcing compliance.

The revocation of the certification of an unfit officer also addresses the issue of problem officers bouncing from department to department. Local departments, facing a difficult time in getting rid of problem cops, sometimes settle for a "geographic transfer." In Arkansas, Elijah Wright, an officer employed by the Helena Police Department, resigned after substantiated complaints of fixing traffic tickets in exchange for sex. After resigning, he applied to work as a deputy with the Pulaski County (Arkansas) Sheriff's Department. During the background check conducted by Pulaski County, three Helena Officers sent letters of recommendation with no mention of the sex incidents. Wright was hired by Pulaski County, and he subsequently "forced women detainees to undress and engage in various sex acts in his presence while he was on duty" (Goldman and Puro 2001).

The International Association of Directors of Law Enforcement Standards and Training has established a National Register of Decertified Officers. As the tool of decertification gains acceptance around the country, this registry could become a check on the re-employment of decertified officers.

State Investigation of Deadly Force Incidents

A second area where state oversight might be productively utilized would be the investigation and potential prosecution of deadly force incidents. In July 2015, New York Governor Andrew Cuomo took that step when he signed an executive order authorizing the state's attorney general to investigate incidents involving the death of a citizen at the hands of the police (New York State Governor's Press Office 2015). Under Cuomo's order, the attorney general will appoint a special prosecutor in these cases whose authority will "supersede in all ways the authority and jurisdiction of a county district attorney to manage, interpret, prosecute or inquire about such incidents" (New York State Governor's Press Office 2015). The order is aimed at minimizing the "public perception of conflict or bias" involved in local prosecutors investigating incidents involving police in their own jurisdiction (New York State Governor's Press Office 2015). The potential conflict inherent in such cases has long been an issue in police–community relations and the move will enhance the legitimacy of these investigations.

Other states should follow this lead. The investigation and prosecution of these cases has, in some instances, become a series of decisions as triggers for disorder and riots. Each step of the criminal justice process—arrest or no arrest, indictment or not, criminal trial and findings of guilt or innocence, and sentence imposed—all become potential flash points. The movement of this process out of the hands of local officials will enhance the perception of neutrality and fairness. Results will be viewed with less of the suspicion and mistrust accompanying local prosecution.

It is unlikely the change will have significant impact on the outcome of these cases. In many ways, the process will be similar to the move toward citizen oversight boards, now a common feature of policing. The belief police were covering up officer misconduct and outside investigations would lead to dramatically different results did not materialize. In fact, studies comparing outside and internal investigation outcomes found the internal investigations "more prone to find misconduct" (Perez and Muir 1995, p. 215). The issue here is less one of outcomes than of ensuring the community of the integrity of the investigation.

State Oversight of Deadly Force Data Reporting

The third area that could be productively addressed by states is collection of data on police deadly force incidents. State-mandated collection would remedy the present dearth of accurate data on police killings. Current data collected by the FBI as part of its national crime reporting system do not provide reliable information on these incidents. The effort to collect these data has fallen victim to bureaucratic bungling, lack of participation by police agencies large and small, and deliberate decisions not to report such deaths. The net result is a serious undercounting of police intervention deaths.

The dimensions of the underreporting are startling. The *Wall Street Journal* secured information on police killings (2007–2012) from 105 of the nation's largest police departments. The figures provided by these agencies were then compared to FBI reported totals for the same agencies for the same time period. The *Journal* found the FBI total 45 percent under the numbers reported by individual agencies. The discrepancy represented about 600 individuals or roughly 100 deaths a year unaccounted for in federal reporting (Barry and Jones 2014). The study documents a major gap between those deaths reported to the FBI and the actual deaths that occurred.

The net result is information so scant as to be nearly irrelevant and of little guidance to policymakers. Two private data collection efforts have the promise of providing a more complete picture. The *Washington Post* has begun tracking police-related deaths with ongoing searches of news sources complimented by reader-provided information. Through the end of 2015, the *Post* tracked 1,000 deaths at the hands of US police officers. That figure represents nearly a doubling of the number of deaths annually reported to the FBI over the previous decade.[2] FBI Director James Comey referred to the current data collection effort by the federal government as "unacceptable" (Kindy et al. 2015).

The Cato Institute has launched a National Police Misconduct Reporting Project (http://www.policemisconduct.net/). The project provides a daily update of all incidents of reported police misconduct. The information on the site includes arrests of police officers, disciplinary action, and more.

With the failure of the FBI crime reporting system to capture data on police deadly force, an effective alternative would be collection of these data by state authorities. The state oversight bodies or police commissions would be in a good position to begin to collect such data. With their certification authority, these organizations have a relationship with every police department in their jurisdiction, and they would be a natural repository for collection of data on police use of force. The data collection could be required under individual state legislation or federal legislation mandating the states collect the information.

Without a mandated requirement to collect this data, government at all levels will continue to struggle with a problem about which they lack the most basic information. In the interim, police and political leaders are in the strange position of relying on entities like the *Washington Post* to provide a more accurate accounting for the most important facet of their own operation.

State Oversight for SWAT Units

A fourth area for state police commission involvement is the regulation of SWAT teams. The origin of SWAT is widely attributed to an incident in Austin, Texas.[3] On August 1, 1966, a man named Charles Whitman, armed with a number of weapons, climbed the Observation Tower on the University of Texas campus and for ninety minutes killed people on the grounds below him. He murdered thirteen people and wounded thirty others before he was slain by the police. This lengthy killing spree highlighted the need for a specialized police unit to respond to snipers, hostage-takers, and other serious incidents beyond the capability of patrol officers. From the first team started by the LAPD in the late 1960s, SWAT teams have proliferated and become a significant presence in US policing. SWAT teams are now found in jurisdictions large and small, and they are involved in an estimated 60,000 missions each year. Journalist Radley Balko has tracked the growth of SWAT teams and reports the FBI alone has fifty-six such teams. Federal agencies that have called on FBI SWAT teams include the "US Fish and Wildlife Service, Consumer Product Safety Commission, National Aeronautics and Space Administration, Department of Education, Department of Health and Human Services, US National Park Service and the Food and Drug Administration" (Balko 2014, p. 308).

The growth of SWAT teams has been driven by the War on Drugs and federal giveaways of military equipment. As SWAT teams have expanded, their role has evolved from response to snipers, barricaded persons, and hostage-takers to an almost exclusive focus on service of search warrants. Even for warrants, the mission has grown from service of high-risk warrants to encompass nearly all search warrants, especially where drug offenses might be involved. With the proliferation of SWAT, their use expanded even beyond warrants. In a 1997 survey of police departments, "twenty percent of the departments he surveyed used SWAT teams or similar units for patrol, mostly in poor, high-crime neighborhoods" (Balko 2014, p. 209).

Unfortunately, as the number of SWAT teams increased and their use by police departments has grown, tragic mistakes as part of their missions have become an all too common occurrence.

In March 2009, a Michigan SWAT team raided the apartment of Derek Copp and his roommate, both students at Grand Valley State University. With a warrant in hand, the raid team attempted to break in a patio door to the apartment. Copp opened the curtains on the door. Startled by what an attorney later described as "an aggressive opening of the curtain," SWAT member Ryan Huizenga shot Copp in the chest. Huizenga was later convicted of reckless discharge of a firearm, served six months' probation, and returned to his department. He was reinstated on the SWAT team (Balko 2013).

In a 2010 incident in Detroit, a SWAT raid resulted in the accidental shooting of seven-year-old Aiyana Stanley-Jones. Officers were searching for her father, who was wanted on a murder charge. Similar to the Copp incident, the SWAT officer who shot the girl attributed it to an accidental discharge. After two trials on felony manslaughter charges, both resulting in hung juries, the officer was found guilty of a misdemeanor count of careless discharge. Sentenced to six months' probation, the officer has returned to duty and remains a member of the SWAT team (Burns 2015).

Despite the high-risk situations and the additional weaponry involved in SWAT operations, few states have developed standards for SWAT teams. The most comprehensive standards for training and deployment of SWAT teams are voluntary, developed by the National Tactical Officers' Association.[4] A few states, California and New York among them, have developed training and operational guidelines for SWAT officers and teams. The California standards are voluntary, referred to as "Guidelines and Recommendation" (California POST 2005). New York State, through its Municipal Police Training Council, has a program that certifies individual SWAT operators and agency teams (New York State Division of Criminal Justice Service n.d.).

With few exceptions, states have left the management and operation of SWAT teams entirely within the purview of individual agencies. The majority of these agencies likely do a good job of screening potential SWAT officers, training both preservice and in-service, and managing the difficult tactical situations from hostage-takers to high-risk search warrants. The fact that most SWAT teams operate without the sort of problems described earlier does not preclude the necessity for increased state regulation. The heavy weaponry and equipment, high-risk situations, and the tactical expertise required all argue for more regulation, not less. The voluntary standards promulgated by the National Tactical Officers Association represent an excellent starting point for states seeking reasonable regulation of military operations on American streets.

End the War on Drugs

For policymakers concerned with addressing police–community relations, efforts to end the fifty-year War on Drugs should be a priority. Michelle Alexander, author of *The New Jim Crow*, describes the War on Drugs as a machine of mass incarceration. Statistics bear out her observation. The United States imprisons more of its citizens than does any other nation in the world, and that fact falls most heavily on the black community. African Americans make up 13 percent of the US population and use drugs at rates similar to whites. But they represent 30 percent of those arrested for drug violations and nearly 40 percent of those in federal prison on drug law convictions (Drug Policy Alliance n.d.). The arrest rate for marijuana offenses is telling. In 2013, despite similar use rates, African Americans were four times more likely to be arrested on marijuana charges than were whites. An ACLU report noted the "War on Marijuana has largely been a war on people of color" (ACLU 2013, p. 21).

Incarceration rates are just the tip of the iceberg. Traffic stops are the most common context for police and citizen interaction, yet statistics show black and white drivers with radically different experiences in these stops. While drivers of all races were stopped roughly in proportion to their percentage of the population, black drivers were three times as likely as white drivers to be searched. Almost twice as many black drivers were arrested during traffic stops as white drivers. White drivers were more likely to receive a warning and black drivers more likely to be ticketed during traffic stops (Eith and Burose 2011).

The disparity raises concerns, and the picture grows bleaker when considering urban areas and looking specifically at the experience of young black men. Skogan found 70 percent of young African American men in Chicago reported being stopped by the police, compared to an average of 20 percent for all Chicago residents (Flexon, Lurigio, and Greenleaf 2009, p. 185). Removing young African

American men from the general population figures makes the discrepancy even larger. Other studies have come to similar conclusions.

New York City has perhaps the most aggressive and certainly the most high-profile "stop and frisk" program in the country. Program statistics provided indicate a wide racial disparity in the stops, particularly when population figures are pared down to young African American men. In an analysis of the NYPD data, the New York Civil Liberties Union noted, "Though they account for only 4.7 percent of the city's population, black and Latino males between the ages of 14–24 accounted for 40.6 percent of the stops in 2012" (New York Civil Liberties Union 2013). In 2012, the number of stops of young African American men neared "the entire city population of young black men" (New York Civil Liberties Union 2013).

There is debate about the meaning of the racial disparity found in these statistics. In a study of the data, the Rand Corporation, using a different set of benchmarks, found the racial disparity much smaller than the raw figures suggest (Ridgeway 2007).

Regardless of the wide variation in interpretation of the figures, in 2013 federal judge Shira Scheindlin ruled that the stop and frisk program violated the constitutional rights of minority citizens, stating the city had been "deliberately indifferent" to police officers illegally detaining and frisking minority residents on the streets over many years (New York Times Editorial Board 2013).

New York is hardly alone in its practice of aggressively stopping young black men in high-crime neighborhoods. Stopping a large number of people in pedestrian or traffic stops under the goal of crime suppression and getting drugs off the street would be described as aggressive proactive policing by a lot of officers. A consensual stop, which may not feel consensual to the citizen, is a tactic out of the same playbook. From the police point of view, the small percentage of stops that actually end with an arrest is perceived as a minor inconvenience to the overwhelming number of people stopped. Citizens, particularly black Americans, experience these stops differently. The tactics in some neighborhoods result in people "being stopped without reason scores of times a year. These unconstitutional stops," Scheindlin wrote, "have exacted a 'human toll' in demeaning and humiliating law-abiding citizens" (New York Times Editorial Board 2013). These repeated experiences, even when done with the utmost in police sensitivity and politeness, leave a residue of mistrust and anger that has a corrosive effect on police efforts at community engagement. Fighting the drug war has brought the police into the lives of black Americans, particularly young men, with an intensity that undercuts the very notion of a free society. Action at the federal and state level bringing an end to the drug war would be the most significant step toward transitioning the police from heavy-handed enforcers to partners in public safety.

Get Police Out of the Revenue Business

In July 2015, University of Cincinnati Police Officer Ray Tensing made a traffic stop on a car driven by Samuel Dubose. Tensing stopped him because his car did not have the state-required front license plate. After some conversation, Tensing asked Dubose to exit the car, but Dubose began to pull away, and Tensing shot him in the head, an incident captured on the officer's body cam. The Hamilton County prosecutor, in a press conference announcing a murder charge against Tensing, described the lack of a front license plate as a "chicken crap" offense.

The prosecutor's colorful description could be applied to a lot more than the front plate ordinance. The encyclopedia of equipment and traffic violations under state and local laws across the country are less aimed at public safety than they are at local government revenue. The Department of Justice, in its review of the Ferguson Police Department, noted "City and police leadership pressure officers to write citations, independent of any public safety need, and rely on citation productivity to fund the City budget" (Department of Justice 2015, p. 10). Responding to supervisory pressure, Ferguson officers routinely issued multiple tickets on the same stop—in one instance, an officer issued fourteen citations in a single traffic stop (Department of Justice 2015, p. 11).

Some police officers view a large quantity of traffic stops as good, aggressive policing. The prosecutor's description of the front license plate violation as "chicken crap" drew immediate reaction from some officers. John Burke, a retired Cincinnati officer and head of a Southwest Ohio Drug Task Force, stated that the prosecutor "has no concept of how many of these so-called 'chicken-crap' stops result in seizures of contraband and felony arrests. Timothy McVeigh, responsible for the Oklahoma City bombing, is a prime example. He was stopped for a license plate violation" (Burke 2015).

Burke's comments reflect the conviction that minor traffic stops sometimes provide the opening wedge to more serious offenses. The drug interdiction effort makes extensive use of this tactic, similar to stop and frisk. These efforts occasionally lead to arrests or citations for driving under suspension or without insurance. Sometimes they lead to drug and/or weapons charges and suspects with open felony warrants.

The success gained from these stops must be balanced against the often unseen costs. Police officers know that most drivers, if followed for even a short period of time, will be in violation of some ordinance. The stops are legal, and for the officer practicing "proactive" policing, the larger picture is blurred. Much of the traffic enforcement under the heading of proactive policing is the same as stop-and-frisk tactics extended to vehicle stops. When the stop involves a white police officer and an African American, racial mistrust may become a factor in the citizen's perception of the encounter. In the same fashion as stop and frisk, ordinary law-abiding citizens may find the experience unsettling and demeaning and leave the encounter with a frustration and anger that erodes police legitimacy.

Reform Civil Asset Forfeiture

Long a staple of the War on Drugs, asset forfeiture by government at all levels has turned constitutional due process on its head. Governments have used the program as a cash machine on the backs of its citizens. Abuses across the country are well documented, but the city of Philadelphia has put itself in the asset forfeiture hall of shame.

The numbers are staggering. In the ten years from 2002 to 2012, "the Philadelphia District Attorney's Office seized and forfeited over 3,000 vehicles, nearly 1,200 homes and other real estate properties and $44 million in cash" (Sibilla 2014). Philadelphia takes in $6 million each year in asset forfeiture. An interesting comparison is Los Angeles County which takes in $1.2 million despite a population six times larger (Sibilla 2014).

Chris Sourovelis is one Philadelphia citizen caught in the city's cash grab. Sourovelis's son was arrested for selling $40 worth of marijuana outside the family home. The son went to court; with a clean record, he was ordered to rehab. A few days later, while driving his son to rehab, Sourovelis got a call from his wife advising him the police were in the house, seizing it under asset forfeiture. As a *Forbes* magazine article noted, authorities can "forfeit a property if it's found to 'facilitate' a crime, no matter how tenuous the connection" (Sibilla 2014). The law not only turns due process upside down by reversing the innocent-until-proven-guilty presumption, it allows innocent people to be punished for the crimes of others. Sourovelis's case caught the attention of the Institute of Justice, which has filed a class-action lawsuit against the city.

Discussion

State legislators across the country have responded to the crisis in policing with a variety of proposed legislative action. Mandating body-cams and increased training are two of the most popular proposals. Twenty states have proposals pending that would mandate training on racial bias. Legislators in several states have proposed increased collection of police force data. Maryland passed a measure establishing behavioral health units as part of police agencies in the Baltimore area (Breitenback 2015).

Many police officers and political leaders will bristle at the notion of expanded regulation of police departments. Although the exact components of state regulation can and should be a matter for vigorous debate and discussion, the right and the responsibility of the state to impose regulation on police goes without question. No other profession has the power and responsibility embedded in policing. That unique level of authority demands a high level of accountability and control.

In a similar fashion, local prosecutors will fight attempts to move police shooting cases into the hands of special prosecutors. In these cases, the importance of transparency and fairness trumps the control of local officials.

An unfortunate facet of US policing has been the failure to discipline and fire bad cops. The cases of officers covering up the wrongdoing of colleagues casts a shadow on every officer and feeds the perception that police view themselves as above the law. When officers act in a criminal and abusive fashion, they harm the legitimacy of the entire profession. Every profession is subject to outside control and regulation, and police are no different. When, for a variety of reasons, police departments fail to discipline officers, particularly in excessive force incidents, a higher authority needs to step in. The certification and licensing authority of states makes them an obvious choice.

Reporting of force incidents is an area demanding immediate attention. The fact that the national police community is unable to accurately state how many citizens die at the hands of the police is unacceptable. It is embarrassing that legislative leaders struggling with the issue of police and deadly force have to rely on the media, the *Washington Post* in particular, for an accurate count of these deaths. The lack of accuracy in what is arguably the most crucial aspect of policing reflects poorly on the profession and tends to validate wild speculation about the true numbers of people killed. Legislative action requiring reporting these deaths to state authorities should be implemented. Each state could pass those numbers onto the federal government. For those agencies reluctant to comply, decertification of their officers, starting with the chief, would provide a necessary incentive.

Although data collection on police use of force should be a priority for state governments, the year-long study by the *Washington Post* should put to rest the notion of an out-of-control police profession. A review of the *Post*'s findings discovered "The police use force mainly to protect human life, the use of force against unarmed suspects is rare, and the use of force against black Americans is largely proportional to their share of the violent crime rate" (French 2015). The review found that shootings of black men by white police officers constituted only about 4 percent of total police shootings (French 2015).

Statistics do not matter when shooting deaths like that of twelve-year-old Tamir Rice in Cleveland or sixteen-year-old Laquan McDonald in Chicago occur. Community and police leaders must respond in a transparent fashion that ensures an impartial and timely investigation and, where warranted, criminal and/or administrative consequences for the police officer. A year-long investigation and the withholding of the video, as in the case of McDonald, only strengthen the belief in the community that officials are involved in a cover-up. This episode sorely damaged the legitimacy of the police and widened the trust gap.

A difficult challenge is ending the War on Drugs. The millions of citizen stops, in cars, on bicycles, and on foot; the searches, some legal and some questionable; and mass incarceration are largely the architecture of the War on Drugs. Dismantling the drug war machine, piece by piece, is under way with the national movement for marijuana legalization a crucial step.

Bolder action is required. Decriminalizing drug possession offenses, expanding drug treatment, and allowing police to concentrate on major traffickers would reduce the intrusive presence of police officers searching for drugs in the cars, homes, and pockets of innocent citizens. Ending the War on Drugs will go a long way in reducing what journalist Travis Smiley describes as "predatory policing" (Smiley

2015, p. 39). The abuses in asset forfeiture and the whole notion of policing for profit cries out for reform. The blatant use of police as revenue agents for local governments is an area needing attention. Ferguson is a notable example, but those who believe these tactics are limited to one locale are deluded. The DOJ Report on the Ferguson Police Department noted police view residents, especially African Americans, "less as constituents to be protected than as . . . sources of revenue" (Marcus 2014). *Washington Post* writer Ruth Marcus noted, "Forget community policing. This is community fleecing, with an ugly racial element" (Marcus 2014).

A combination of police reform and an end to the War on Drugs would have significant effect in easing the relations between police and African Americans. These changes are likely to be incremental. The failure of institutional change makes more important the necessity for individual police officers and individual police departments to take action. The nearly 700,000 US police officers, acting every day with compassion and treating the people they encounter with dignity, can make a major contribution toward finally closing the racial divide.

Notes

1. It is unclear in this case (and others like it) why criminal charges were not lodged against the officers.

2. By tracking only police shooting deaths, the *Post* study undercounts the number of people killed in police encounters. The well-publicized death of Eric Garner in New York City following a chokehold is an example of incidents not caught in the database.

3. In 1964, the Philadelphia Police Department created a "Special Weapons and Tactics" team to respond to bank robberies. The LAPD is generally credited with the formation of the first unit as the forerunner of modern SWAT teams.

4. The NTOA Standards for SWAT teams are found at https://ntoa.org /massemail/swatstandards.pdf

11

Transforming
Fear to Trust

It is hard to overstate the intimacy of the contact between the police and the community. Policemen deal with people when they are both most threatening and most vulnerable, when they are angry, when they are frightened, when they are desperate, when they are drunk, when they are violent, or when they are ashamed.

—Task Force Report on Law Enforcement (1967)

There are two things cops hate—the way things are and change.

—Sue Rahr, former sheriff of Kings County, WA

When it has to do with race and the police, there are always very hard lines drawn.

—Ben Watson[1]

Each episode of racial violence has led to task forces and study commissions whose recommendations ended up gathering dust on government and library shelves. A cursory review of those reports confirms the long-standing nature of the gap between police and the African American community. The Chicago Commission Report on the 1919 riot notes the lack of "faith in the white police force" and "the stimulus of the policeman's conduct" as factors in the rioting (Chicago Commission on Race Relations 1922, pp. 5–6). Leaders of the black community reported that "discrimination in arrest was a principal cause of widespread and long-standing distrust. Whether justified or not, this feeling was actual and bitter" (Chicago Commission on Race Relations 1922, p. 34).

The level of "faith" in the police did not appear to have improved much in the fifty years between the 1919 Chicago riot and the riots of the 1960s. After those events, the President's Commission on Law Enforcement recommended "greatly enlarged and strengthened police-community relations units, improved procedures for handling citizen complaints, [and] better screening to eliminate candidates for the police force who are biased" (Major Cities Chiefs Association et al. 2015, p. 15). The report also noted that black Americans "were growing increasingly sensitive to being frequently stopped and questioned or arrested for minor crimes" (Major Cities Chiefs Association et al., p. 15). Today, much of the content of the 1960s reports could be cut and pasted into the task force and commission reports that will undoubtedly follow the disorders in Ferguson, Baltimore, and those yet to come.

The responsibility for changing this long-standing tension between police and African American constituents rests primarily with police officers and the departments they work for. There is no shortage of ideas. Some specific recommendations are covered here.

Traffic Stops and Community Safety

Traffic stops by police typically have three purposes: to provide a deterrent effect to reckless driving, to generate revenue for local government, and to act as a wedge for arrests on more serious offenses.

Traffic stops for the purpose of revenue enhancement are at best ethically questionable. US citizens are constitutionally guaranteed freedom from unwarranted government intrusion, and traffic stops without a public safety purpose erodes that freedom. When citizens perceive these stops as money grabs by local government, police legitimacy suffers.

Traffic stops to enhance public safety mean enforcement at locations with high risk for accident injuries. Officers writing tickets simply to make numbers will choose "fishing holes" where easy pickings are available. Citing somebody for rolling through a stop sign at 3:00 a.m. contributes little or nothing to public safety and is likely a ticket written to keep police supervisors happy.

Making a volume of traffic stops as proactive or aggressive policing is a more difficult dilemma. For officers, every traffic stop represents the potential of a dangerous suspect, the earlier noted stop of

Timothy McVeigh as a prime example. The stop could be a drug trafficker with a trunk full of heroin and money. The stop could be a felony suspect with an open warrant. The key to these stops are minor offenses, a headlight out, a loud muffler, or failing to use a turn signal. Each stop represents the chance to check the driver for warrants, observe drugs or guns in the car, and/or secure permission for a search of the trunk. The practices are a form of police lottery. The odds are against winning on each individual stop, but the more tickets purchased, the greater the chance of a prize.

The relationship of aggressive policing to crime control and public safety is nebulous at best. There are clearly a lot of instances where these stops lead to significant arrests or drug seizures. Measuring the hidden costs is more difficult. Particularly in an urban area, a high volume of stops may involve young African American men, the overwhelming majority of whom have never committed any offense. Yet their perception is they are treated like criminals, and they are likely to view the stop as racial profiling. One African American witness speaking to the President's Commission noted, "By the time you are 17, you have been stopped and frisked a dozen times" (President's Task Force on 21st Century Policing, p. 11). The loss of police legitimacy and the resulting resentment and mistrust stemming from these experiences are not as visible as numbers of arrests and drug seizures.

An emphasis on aggressive policing may have been a factor in the 2015 traffic stop leading to the shooting death of Samuel DuBose by a University of Cincinnati (UC) police officer. In late 2013, there were a number of highly publicized assaults and robberies of UC students in the area surrounding the campus. In response, UC President Santa Ono wrote a letter to Hamilton County judges asking for sentencing to "send a clear, forceful and reverberating message to criminals and the broader community that predatory targeting of UC students will have severe consequences" (WLWT-TV 2013).

At the same time, UC police were ordered to patrol neighborhoods surrounding the campus in an effort to suppress crime against students. They responded by dramatically increasing traffic enforcement off-campus.[2] In the first six months of 2014, UC officers wrote more tickets than the total for 2013 and three times the number written in 2012. Analysis of the tickets found racial disparity with 62 percent of the 2014 tickets going to African Americans, up from 43 percent going to African Americans in 2012. Confronted with the disparity, the UC police chief described himself "horrified" at the figures[3], and the campus police were ordered to stop writing tickets off campus (Williams 2015).

There is no easy solution to this dilemma. Good supervision will help by insisting that all issued tickets reflect a public safety hazard. Equipment violations, broken taillight, and so on should result in warning tickets, allowing time to fix the problem and dropping the citation once the issue is remedied. Careful tracking of any racial disparity has to be done, and any indication of bias or profiling should be quickly addressed.

One concrete change suggested would add a requirement for written consent prior to any consensual search. This would provide a check on abuses in the voluntary search area. This action would also put citizen rights in a more prominent light in a tactic with weak constitutional underpinnings.

The War on Drugs is a factor in these traffic stops. The majority of the stops under the banner of "proactive" policing result from an emphasis on drug interdiction and seizure of drugs, and drug money is the major prize sought. Ending the drug war and reforming asset forfeiture laws would remove much of the incentive underlying these stops.

Stop and Frisk

Much of the discussion on traffic stops is applicable to pedestrian stops. The two types of stops most concerning are Terry stops, where reasonable suspicion exists, and consensual stops. Proactive policing attempts to transition these stops into searches. A high volume of these stops and the ensuing searches will inevitably turn up some drugs and weapons. A review of the 2012 statistics from the NYPD stop and frisk effort revealed that 2 percent of the searches found weapons. The most common arrest following these stops was marijuana possession (Flatrow 2013).

Now that a federal judge has ruled the NYPD program unconstitutional, some guidelines for police officers are crucial. The probability of these interactions ending up as online videos suggests clear justification for the search should be articulated for all seen and unseen recordings. If a consensual stop is made, the officer needs to loudly and clearly state the citizen is free to walk away. If a consensual stop develops into a search, a written consent form should be signed.

Legalities aside, the most crucial element here is the demeanor and verbalizations by the police. A respectful and polite approach minimizes the tension inherent in the stops. Journalist Heather MacDonald, a staunch supporter of the NYPD stop and frisk program, notes, "a perennial problem; how to prevent officers from developing a rude and hardened demeanor . . . Keeping cops polite would go a long way toward tamping down resentment against them" (MacDonald 2013).

Moving officers out of the proactive policing style characterized by interdiction-focused traffic stops and aggressive stop and frisk will require change in the traditional incentives for officer behavior. If police leaders truly want officers to participate in community engagement, they will need to reconfigure evaluation and promotional measures to stress engagement and community policing skills rather than numerical measures tracking numbers of tickets written and arrests made.

SWAT Team Management

Police officers are given tremendous authority and responsibility in our society. When that authority is magnified by the heavy weaponry and military tactics used by SWAT teams, the need for clear policy, ongoing training, and intensive command and control is paramount. With the national proliferation of SWAT teams, the mission has expanded, along with the potential for misuse. In 2007, as Texas hold'em poker tournaments gained in popularity around the country, some local police departments responded with SWAT raids on the tournaments. Balko reports SWAT raids launched on poker games in Maryland, Texas, North Carolina, South Carolina, and California. In 2007, Dallas authorities used SWAT to raid a Veterans of Foreign Wars Hall sponsoring a charitable poker event (Balko 2014, p. 282).

Poker games were not the only target for aggressive SWAT teams. In 2010, over a period of three months, Orange County, Florida, officers raided a number of African American barber shops, holding barbers and customers at gunpoint while the shops were searched. In total, thirty-seven arrests were made, thirty-four of them for barbering without a license (Balko 2014, p. 284). Balko notes that the officers doing the raids did not have search warrants, but instead conducted raids based on suspicion of violation of administrative regulations under the Florida Department of Business and Professional Regulation (Balko 2014, p. 284).

The tactic of using SWAT for enforcement of state administrative regulations was not limited to barber shops. In 2010, a SWAT team in Connecticut raided a bar after complaints of underage drinking (Balko 2014, p. 284). In addition to raids on bars, SWAT teams have also raided fraternity and sorority parties across the country under the pretext of liquor violations.

An attorney representing poker players arrested in a South Carolina SWAT raid captured the police state nature of the raids. "The typical police raid of these games . . . is to literally burst into a home in SWAT gear with guns drawn and treat poker players like a bunch of high-level drug dealers. Using the taxpayers' resources for such useless Gestapo-like tactics is more of a crime than is playing of the game" (Kinnard 2009).

With the lack of any real state oversight and the easy provision of military equipment from the federal government, the abuses listed here will continue to occur. Raids on bars and barber shops where customers are confronted at gunpoint are high risk for the accidental discharge incidents documented in a number of botched SWAT raids. There are other costs to these raids that are less apparent.

Forcing citizens to the floor at gunpoint—whether customers at a barber shop, poker players, or art patrons in a 2015 raid at the Contemporary Art Institute of Detroit (CAID)—constitutes a police use of force only the most ardent supporter would describe as constitutionally reasonable. The potential abuses in these raids were captured in the Detroit CAID incident.

Attendees at the 2008 event were shocked when a contingent of Detroit Police SWAT members burst into the gallery, ordering the patrons to their knees, with one man, attorney Paul Kaiser, kicked in the face for failing to move quickly enough. The car keys of all those present were confiscated, and over forty cars were towed and released only after payment of a $1,000 administrative fee. The stated purpose of the raid was that CAID lacked proper licenses for drinking and dancing (Stillman 2013).

Lacking the barest regulatory oversight, use of SWAT teams has been left to individual police departments, in some cases acting without significant internal control. Without the possibility of any substantial state oversight in the near future, decisions on creation of SWAT teams, their training, and criteria for SWAT deployment are in the hands of local police leaders. In the face of free military equipment, saying no to SWAT may become a politically difficult decision. However, the consequences for police liability are multiplied with the additional weaponry, and the use of SWAT in anything but the most serious of circumstances carries significant risks.

When SWAT teams raid barber shops, holding people at gunpoint, and then cite the shops for "barbering without a license," they risk destroying their own credibility. When a police department becomes the butt of citizen humor, it has dug itself a legitimacy hole that will be difficult to overcome. Using SWAT to raid college parties, poker games, art galleries, and barber shops invites citizen ridicule, sabotaging efforts at community engagement.

When a SWAT team acts in a constitutionally questionable fashion, they further undermine their credibility. When citizens perceive police action as legally out of bounds, and where these actions are directed against black people or black businesses, mistrust of the police festers. That mistrust begins to creep into the everyday encounters between police and African American citizens.

Norm Stamper, former chief of police in Seattle, suggests that police departments "prohibit SWAT operations for anything other than school shootings, armed hostage situations and other immediate crises when negotiations fail and lives are at stake" (Stamper 2014). Following this recommendation would put SWAT teams back to their original purpose, prevent the constitutional abuses inherent in some deployments, and recast SWAT teams as heroic professionals responding to extremely critical events.

Police Operations: Body-Cams

Perhaps the most widely agreed-on change in policing is the requirement for officer body cameras, recording citizen–police encounters. Video technology has advanced to the point where miniature cameras can be attached to a collar, a lapel, or even glasses. In theory, the presence of the camera has an impact on both officer and citizen behavior.

The body-cams are an evolution from the in-car cameras, or dash-cams, installed on thousands of police vehicles during the 1990s. The impact of the dash-cams was significant. A 2002 study by the International Association of Chiefs of Police documented multiple effects of dash-cams. Many officers reported the cameras were instrumental in improving officer safety, not for their presence during a traffic stop or citizen encounter, but for the officer's later viewing of the video and self-critique of safety tactics.

Another major area of impact was officer behavior during these encounters. Officers noted the awareness of the camera, and the possibility of supervisor review meant an increased focus on professionalism.

The presence of the cameras also had a significant impact on citizen complaints. In a written survey of officers, 96 percent reported citizen complaints against them were unfounded following video review by supervisors. In a related finding, officers reported in roughly half the cases that once the citizen was made aware a video record was available, the complaint was dropped (Westphal 2004).

There is emerging evidence that body-cams, with their ability to capture a much broader slice of police encounters, are having similarly positive effects. Under the auspices of the Police Foundation, a study done on body-cams in Rialto, California, suggests the body-cams result in a significant reduction in both use of force and citizen complaints. The study found a more than 50 percent reduction in use-of-force incidents when compared with control conditions and a nearly tenfold reduction in citizen complaints (Farrar 2013).

The dash-cams and body-cams both represent huge steps in technology to provide significant transparency in police operations. Although there has been some initial resistance to body-cams reported, the positive experience with dash-cams should allay some of these concerns. There are issues with implementation of body-cams, notably protection of the privacy of citizens caught on video in what may likely be described as a public record. The cost for data storage of the digital records generated by body-cams has been an issue for some departments. On balance, for police leaders seeking to improve their department's legitimacy, purchase of body-cams would be a priority investment.

Police Operations: Training

Police officers today are faced with challenges unknown to law enforcement even a decade ago. Mass shootings, international terrorism, cybercrimes, immigration issues, and growing drug abuse and mental health problems confront police on a daily basis. Training may well be the key piece in helping officers meet these challenges, and the importance of community engagement has to be incorporated into training as a central theme.

Sue Rahr, executive director of the Washington State Criminal Justice Training Commission, and a retired sheriff, is reinventing police training. Rahr began her examination of training in 2012 by asking a question:

> "Why are we training police officers like soldiers?" Although police officers wear uniforms and carry weapons, the similarity ends there. The missions and rules of engagement are completely

different. The soldier's mission is that of a warrior: to conquer. The rules of engagement are decided before the battle. The police officer's mission is that of a guardian: to protect. The rules of engagement evolve as the incident unfolds. Soldiers must follow orders. Police officers must make independent decisions. Soldiers come into communities as an outside, occupying force. Guardians are members of the community, protecting from within. (Rahr 2014)

The training model developed by Rahr and her colleagues hinges on two concepts. First is an emphasis on the ideal expressed by Sir Robert Peel, the father of modern policing, when he said, "the police are the people, and the people are the police." Rahr notes the increasing militarization of policing has led to a police "culture and mindset more like warriors at war with the people we are sworn to protect and serve" (Rahr and Rice 2015).

The second hinge is a focus on the role of police as guardians of constitutional rights. Rahr rightly notes, "Constitutional rights are now viewed by some, including some police, as an impediment to the public safety mission. Sadly, many have forgotten that protecting constitutional rights is the mission of police in a democracy" (Rahr and Rice 2015).

Building on these key tenets, Rahr set about changing the curriculum and the training environment. A display case in the lobby of the Police Academy, previously filled with "tools of the trade with a consistent theme of warriors, battles and survival" has been transformed. Rahr observed the lack of emphasis on constitutional policing. "Noticeably absent from both the physical environment and curriculum was any reference to service and the noble and historical role of policing in a democracy" (Rahr and Rice 2015). Rahr replaced the lobby display with a large mural of the US Constitution, under the heading "In these Halls . . . Training the Guardians of Democracy" (Rahr and Rice 2015).

In service of the importance of effective community engagement, Rahr stressed the use of physical force as a last resort and emphasized verbal skills and deescalation tactics as alternatives to physical control. She continued the emphasis in academy training on defensive skills and physical fitness. Behavioral strategies and force decision making has been woven throughout the training to reflect the reality of policing.

The importance of training can hardly be overstated. Research on police training has not been encouraging. A report by the Major Cities Chiefs Association and other groups notes, "We have every reason to believe that existing training in academies and the experience of field training is also unintentionally degrading social performance. That is, our existing efforts are not maintaining status quo competencies and they aren't likely improving performance. This should get everyone's attention" (Major Cities Chiefs Association et al. 2015, p. 65).

A research project is under way following officers trained in Rahr's academy. The study will attempt to confirm if the new emphasis has an impact on officers' field performance. The five-year study will measure whether officers trained in the new philosophy are more likely to use crisis intervention and deescalation skills than those trained under the old warrior philosophy.

Police Transparency and Search Warrants

Transparency is a concept appearing regularly in discussions of police reform. Use of force investigations are priority in the discussion, but traffic stop data, arrest and crime statistics, agency polices, hiring practices, and agency diversity are only a few of the items police leaders could make readily available in the service of transparency. A topic not often mentioned is search warrants.

As part of the drug war and with the proliferation of SWAT teams, the number of search warrants served by police has escalated. Very few agencies track or make available information on numbers of search warrants, the number of times SWAT is used to serve warrants, or results of the warrant. After a highly publicized botched SWAT raid in Maryland, the state legislature passed a law in 2009 mandating collection of information on search warrants. Statistics released under that effort highlight the problem. Figures showed that 94 percent of the total SWAT deployments were for search or arrest warrants. Only the remaining 6 percent represented the type of critical incidents— hostage-takers, barricaded persons, and bank robberies—that SWAT was designed for. In Prince George's County alone, the first six months' figures found SWAT teams forced entry 100 times into private homes for nonserious, nonviolent offenses (Balko 2014, pp. 316–17). Transparency on search warrants is an issue going beyond the police. The constitutional check on search warrant abuse is judges who must review and approve the warrant. Unfortunately, this is a responsibility taken lightly by some judges. A study done of the warrant process in a number of American cities found judges spent an average of "two minutes and forty-eight seconds reviewing warrant affidavits prior to nearly 100% approval" (Balko 2014, p. 185).

A publicly available database on warrants, which tracks warrant activity from start to finish, would move the search warrant process out of the dark and into the light of police transparency.

Managing the Internal Culture

David Couper, former chief of the Madison, Wisconsin Police Department, made an eloquent comment on police organizations when he noted, "Some of the people we were trying to attract into a police career were currently in business, law, social work, or teaching. And most of them wouldn't choose to remain in a police department that ran like an 18th century British Warship" (Rahr and Rice 2015).

Couper's comment resonates with a lot of rank-and-file police officers. A comment heard repeatedly in discussions with police officers on stress in police work is that the major stress is not in the street but in the stationhouse. Although poor management is a chronic complaint by people in nearly every organization, in police departments, lousy management has a tendency to creep outside and contaminate engagement with the community. The President's Task Force on 21st Century Policing (p. 4) noted that "officers who feel respected by their organizations are more likely to bring this respect into their interactions with the people they serve."

The overriding mission of the department is one that has to be shared by all officers and other employees. Strong cooperative relationships throughout a department, in the same fashion as relationships in the community, results in a more effective team effort directed at public safety.

The converse is also true. Poor management will impede the department's efforts at community engagement, making the policing effort even more challenging. A 1995 study of Community Policing in Chicago identified supervisory practices known to sabotage efforts at community policing. They included:

- Bean counting on performance evaluations
- Micromanaging officers' efforts
- Favoritism in assignments
- Ruling through fear and intimidation. (Geller and Swanger 1995)

The poor supervisory practices listed are hardly breaking news, nor is the list complete. Nearly everyone with even minimal time in work organizations could make additions. The challenge for police managers is establishing a workplace focused on and committed to engagement and community policing.

Improving Departmental Operations to Prevent Disorder

The "Patterns and Practices" investigations done by the Department of Justice, most recently in Ferguson, represents a high-cost process of departmental reform implemented after the damage is done.

These efforts, sometimes coming postriot, include court actions, federal monitoring teams, and a lengthy public airing of departmental problems, the sum of which drives the department's legitimacy account into the red. The changes forced on departments under DOJ mandates may have long-term positive outcomes, as the Collaborative Agreement in Cincinnati demonstrates. However, the whole process argues for a significant effort to assist local departments in implementing changes prior to any disorder.

Making assistance available to local departments could be done under the auspices of organizations such as the Police Executive Research Foundation, the International Chiefs of Police Association, the National Fraternal Order of Police, and the National Organization of Black Law Enforcement Executives. A collaborative effort among the organizations listed might be even more effective.

The vision is a group of three to five policing experts working on-site with local authorities and police officials; reviewing policy and procedure, traffic stop data, and use of force data; meeting with community members; and spending time in the field with police officers. The goal of the effort is an individualized plan for the department *and* the community aimed at a high level of engagement and a joint problem solving effort targeted at crime and disorder problems.

The willingness of a police department to undergo this process, in cooperation with their community, would provide a significant investment in community legitimacy, providing a riot immunization effect.

Funding for such an effort, even directed at a modest number of departments each year, would need to be made available through the federal or state governments. It is likely many of the police "experts" needed would be willing to assist for minimal compensation to keep the costs low.[4] Providing a modest level of funding for a preventive effort would save the major expenses involved in reform efforts undertaken after disorder has occurred.

A National Police Service Academy

There is wide agreement lack of diversity, particularly at the leadership level, remains an impediment to effective police relations with black citizens. A National Police Service Academy, modeled after the military academies at West Point, Annapolis, and Colorado Springs, could become a training ground for the police leaders of the future.

A four-year program leading to an undergraduate degree and covering policing, criminal justice, and legal issues, with a strong emphasis on leadership, could create a stream of highly skilled police leaders who would be available to begin in middle management positions across the country. Significant time would be devoted to internships working as an officer in major metropolitan areas, providing a foundation of experience to complement academic training. One option might be locating the academy on the grounds at Quantico, where these officers could work and train along with FBI agents. Diversity in admissions would be a priority, and standards would be high. Like those attending service academies, all incoming freshman would make a commitment of five years of police service following graduation. Every student could be sponsored by a police department in their own community, with a guaranteed position on graduation.

The need for leadership training is widely recognized. One recommendation of the President's Task Force is for "A national postgraduate institute of policing for senior executives . . . with a standardized curriculum preparing participants to lead agencies in the 21st century" (President's Task Force on 21st Century Policing, p. 4). Although there is no dispute over the need for leadership training for current police executives, the establishment of a National Police Service Academy would provide a cadre of future leaders. A logical step would be housing a postgraduate institute as recommended within the proposed national academy.

A National Police Service Academy addresses two important goals in police reform: diversity, with an emphasis on recruitment of motivated and highly qualified African American candidates, and leadership, providing the best executive training available to the police leaders of the future.

Eliminating Racism in the Police Ranks

For police, race remains the number one challenge. The history of racism in the ranks is indisputable. The 1919 Chicago Commission Report noted, "The failure of the police to arrest impartially . . . whether from insufficient effort or otherwise, was a mistake and had a tendency to further incite and aggravate the colored population" (Chicago Commission on Race Relations 1922, p. 36). Police arrests during the rioting also were scrutinized. "Our attention was called strikingly to the fact that at the time of race rioting, the arrests made for rioting by the police of colored rioters were far in excess of the arrests made of white rioters" (Chicago Commission on Race Relations 1922, p. 36).

Almost a century later, the racial disparity decried in 1919 persists. By nearly every measure, African Americans fare more poorly at the hands of the police and the criminal justice system than do their white counterparts. The portion of the disparity attributed to racism is difficult to quantify, but a reasonable observer, looking at the statistics, could hardly deny race as a factor.

It is imperative for police leaders to relentlessly review their own operations and ensure that racism is not a factor in their departments. Individual police officers, no matter what color their skin, need to believe with certainty that racial biases are not influencing their actions. The challenge for police departments across the country is to closely review their agency practices from recruiting to on-the-street performance, ensuring their officers act and perform their duties without bias.

Former police chief Norm Stamper speaks for the majority of police leadership when he advocates "non-negotiable standards for the performance and conduct of each and every police officer," including termination for any "found to be using racial or ethnic slurs" (Stamper 2014).

Improving Social Conditions for Black Americans

The Chicago Commission Report summarized the living conditions of African-Americans in Chicago at that time as "wretched" noting, "The ordinary conveniences, considered necessities by the average white citizen, are often lacking" (Chicago Commission on Race Relations 1922, p. 36).

By the time the Kerner Commission issued its report in 1967, things hardly seemed to have improved. The report stated, "Segregation and poverty have created in the racial ghetto a destructive environment totally unknown to most white Americans" (National Advisory Commission on Civil Disorder 1967, p. 1).

The period from the 1960s to the present has led to marked improvement, but the economic gap between white and black citizens remains substantial. Evidence of the gap's persistence is found in the 2015 President's Task Force Report on Policing. In a report including pages of recommendations for policing, one nonpolice overarching recommendation was listed, and it stated: "The President should promote programs that take a comprehensive and inclusive look at community-based initiatives that address the core issues of poverty, education, health, and safety" (p. 8).

The economic circumstances of black people were seen as factors in rioting in 1919, 1943, and the 1960s and remain part of the current discussion. Conditions in many of the country's African American neighborhoods remain depressed with unemployment, substandard housing, high crime, drug problems, and broken families all part of a socially depressing mix. Just as in earlier eras, these conditions represent the kindling for disorder and rioting easily sparked into flames by police action.

The very persistence of these problems speaks to their difficult nature. There are pockets of success, and over the past century, the tearing down of racial barriers has led to substantial improvement. The tenacity of the racial gap between police and the African American community is evidence of the work yet to be done.

Warriors and Guardians

For US police officers, the failures of the past become the burden of the present. The intense scrutiny faced by the police today is hardly novel. A 1968 task force report on policing noted, "Since this is a time of increasing crime, increasing social unrest and increasing public sensitivity to both, it is a time when police work is peculiarly important, complicated, conspicuous, and delicate" (President's Commission on Law Enforcement and Justice 1968).

Building legitimacy, community engagement, transparency in operations, and a commitment to community policing are all actions leading to improved relations between African Americans and the police. Yet over the past decades, the culture and tactics of police departments have shifted to a more militaristic presence in the community. The fifty-year War on Drugs has been the primary driver of this transition. That shift has led to mass incarceration, an erosion of constitutional rights, and a widening gap between the police and the communities they are sworn to protect.

The vision of police in a democracy is eloquently captured by Plato: "In a republic that honors the core of democracy—the greatest amount of power is given to those called Guardians. Only those with the most impeccable character are chosen to bear the responsibility of protecting the democracy" (quoted in Rahr and Rice 2015).

Unfortunately, today's police officers are too often confronted with the necessity to act as warriors, and the phrase "active shooter" has become common in police work. In a single weekend in spring 2015, police in Chicago responded to thirty-seven shootings. Waco, Texas, police were involved in a shooting battle between motorcycle gangs that left 9 dead, 18 injured, and 179 people arrested. A few weeks earlier, in Garland, Texas, a single officer engaged with two ISIS members wearing body armor and armed with automatic rifles, killing both and saving multiple lives.

The San Bernardino terrorist attack in October 2015 resulted in the deaths of fourteen people. The murderers, armed with multiple weapons and bombs and determined to martyr themselves, were stopped only after an extended firefight, the type of extreme violence becoming all too familiar to US police officers.

With an upsurge in violence afflicting US communities large and small, police increasingly find themselves in violent confrontations. With the threat of violence an inescapable piece of the fabric of police work, there will be occasions when officers must act as warriors, moving with courage and resolve in protection of their life and the lives of others. Between the deaths of Michael Brown in Ferguson and Freddie Gray in Baltimore, over ninety police officers died in the line of duty. Their deaths, in the pursuit of community safety, went mostly unnoticed.

The challenge is daunting. Racial tension remains a stubborn feature of modern life. The task of racial equality is a challenge for the whole nation, but nowhere is there more urgency than in policing.

In meeting the challenge, it should be recognized that the face-to-face community engagement in this effort is crucial. A 2013 review of studies on police legitimacy found "any type of intervention could be used to facilitate legitimacy as long as it includes an opportunity for police to engage in with citizens" (Mazerolle et al. 2013b). Thus, whether implementing a crisis response program, new training on use of force, or a community discussion on race and policing, the key factor is community engagement throughout the process. Those ongoing conversations with members of the public will effectively change the relationship.[5]

Individual police officers, working as both warriors and guardians in the community, acting with compassion and fairness, can erode the historic mistrust separating them from the African American community. The key to making the transition from fear to trust involves daily community engagement, working alongside neighborhood residents, and sharing success in resolving crime and disorder problems. The new relationship holds the promise to finally close the rift between the police and the African American communities they serve.

Notes

1. Watson, a player for the NFL New Orleans Saints, posted a thoughtful short essay on Facebook following the shooting of Michael Brown in Ferguson.

2. Per the Kroll Investigative Report on the Shooting of Sam DuBose, at the moment of the shooting, there were four University of Cincinnati patrol units on duty. Three of the four were engaged in traffic stops. The Kroll Report is available at http://www.uc.edu/content/dam/uc/safety-reform/documents/Kroll%20Report%20of%20Investigation%208.31.2015.pdf.

3. The chief initially denied knowledge of the heavy traffic enforcement by UC officers. Later investigation found he had in fact encouraged the stops. He and his assistant commander were both forced to resign in the spring of 2016.

4. There are a number of self-described experts charging large fees for "police consultation." Careful stewardship of public funds demands thorough vetting of these individuals.

5. Although the program components of the Cincinnati Collaborative have received well-deserved positive reviews, the importance of the ongoing and intensive discussions among members of the public and police officers has been overlooked.

Bibliography

Alcindor, Yamiche, Greg Toppo, Gary Strauss, and John Bacon. "Ferguson Burning after Grand Jury Announcement," *USA Today*, November 25, 2014.

Alexander, Michelle. *The New Jim Crow: Mass Incarceration in the Age of Colorblindness*. New York: New Press, 2010.

Alpert, Geoffrey and Michael Smith. "Police Use of Force Data: Where We Are and Where We Should Be Going." *Police Quarterly* 1, no. 1: 57–58, 1999.

Alpert, Geoffery P., Michael R. Smith, Robert J. Kaminski, Lorie A. Fridell, John MacDonald, and Bruce Kubu. "Police Use of Force, Tasers and other Less Lethal Weapons," NIJ, Research in Brief, May 2011.

American Civil Liberties Union (ACLU). "The War on Marijuana in Black and White—Billions of Dollars Wasted on Racially Biased Arrests," June 1, 2013.

Archives of the Tuskegee Institute. "Lynching Statistics by Year," n.d. http://law2.umkc.edu/faculty/projects/ftrials/shipp/lynchingyear.html.

Ashkenas, Jeremy, and Haeyoun Park. "The Race Gap in America's Police Departments," *New York Times*, September 3, 2014.

Bachhuber, Marcus A., Brendan Saloner, Chinazo O. Cunningham, and Colleen L. Barry. "Medical Cannabis Laws and Opioid Analgesic Overdose Mortality in the United States, 1999–2010," *JAMA Internal Medicine*, 174, no. 10 (2014): 1668–73.

Baeder, Ben. "Zoot Suit Riots: Racism Underlies Week of Violence in Los Angeles," *Los Angeles Daily News*, May 31, 2013.

Balko, Radley. "Raid of the Day—Derrek Copp," *Huffington Post*, May 9, 2013, http://www.huffingtonpost.com.

Balko, Radley. *Rise of the Warrior Cop: The Militarization of America's Police Forces*. New York: Public Affairs, 2014.

Balko, Radley. "An Interview with the Baltimore Cop Who's Revealing All the Horrible Things He Saw on the Job," *Washington Post*, June 25, 2015.

Bapat, Vivek. "3 Ways to Build Brand Equity in the Social Era," *Forbes Magazine*, September 9, 2014.

Barry, Rob, and Coulter Jones. "Hundreds of Police Killings Are Uncounted in Federal Stats," *Wall Street Journal*, December 3, 2014.

Berger, Jonah. *Contagious: Why Things Catch On*. New York: Simon and Schuster, 2013.

Bieck, W., W. Spelman, and T. Sweeney. "The Patrol Function." In William A. Geller, ed., *Local Government Police Management*. Washington, DC: International City Management Association, 1991.

Bigart, Homer. "Newark Riot Deaths at 21 as Negro Sniping Widens." Special to the *New York Times*, July 16, 1967.

Bosman, Julie, and Joseph Goldstein. "Delay in Moving Body Helped Fuel Outrage in Ferguson," *New York Times*, August 24, 2014.

Bradner, Eric. "Obama 'No Excuse' for Violence in Baltimore," CNN, April 28, 2015, http://www.cnn.com/2015/04/28/.

Breitenback, Sarah. "States Pursue Varied Police Reforms Amid National Debate," *Stateline*, Pew Charitable Trusts, June 1, 2015, http://www.pewtrusts.org/en/research-and-analysis/.

Bronson, Peter. *Behind the Lines: The Untold Story of the Cincinnati Riots*. Milford, OH: Chilidog Press, 2006.

Bronson, Peter. "Lessons for Ferguson from Cincinnati's 2001 Riots," *Wall Street Journal*, August 22, 2014.

Brown, J. M., and P. A. Langan. *Policing and Homicide, 1976–98: Justifiable Homicide by Police, Police Officers Murdered by Felons*. Washington, DC: US Bureau of Justice Statistics, 2001.

Bulwa, Demian. "Mehserle Blurted Term of Shock, Witness Says," *San Francisco Chronicle*, January 8, 2011, p. C1.

Bulwa, Demian. "Final Arguments Continue in Mehserle Trial," *San Francisco Chronicle*, January 8, 2011, p. C1.

Bureau of Justice Statistics. "Local Police," US Department of Justice, 2013, http://www.bjs.gov/index.cfm?ty=tp&tid=71.

Burke, John. "Long-time Cop—Deters Is Way Out of Line," *Cincinnati Enquirer*, August 7, 2015.

Burns, Gus. "Officer Who Shot Aiyana Stanley-Jones Won't Face Third Trial," *Michigan Live*, June 28, 2015, http://www.mlive.com/.

California Governor's Commission on the Los Angeles Riots. "Violence in the City—An End or a Beginning," A Report, 1967.

California POST. "SWAT Operational Guidelines and Training Recommendations," 2005, http://lib.post.ca.gov/Publications/swatmanual.pdf.

Cannon, Jack. *Official Negligence, How Rodney King and the Riots Changed Los Angeles and the LAPD*. Boulder, CO: Westview Press, 1999.

Carson, E. M. "Prisoners in 2013," US Dept. of Justice, Bureau of Justice Statistics, September 2014, http://www.bjs.gov/content/pub/pdf/p13.pdf.

Cheh, M. M. "Are Lawsuits an Answer to Police Brutality?" In W. Geller and H. Toch (eds.), *And Justice for All: Understanding and Controlling Police Abuse of Force*, Washington, DC: Police Executive Research Forum, 1995.

Chicago Commission on Race Relations. *The Negro in Chicago: A Study of Race Relations and a Race Riot.* Chicago: University of Chicago Press, 1922.

Cincinnati Enquirer Editorial. "Amid Trying Times, Strengthened by Trust," *Cincinnati Enquirer*, July 29, 2015, p. 6A.

Cincinnati Police Division. "Executive Information Summary Report (2003)," City of Cincinnati, 2003.

City University of New York. "New York City Harlem Riots of 1943," n.d., http://www.baruch.cuny.edu/nycdata/disasters/riots-harlem_1943.html.

Clement, Scott. "Whites Are More Confident Than Ever that Their Local Police Treat Blacks Fairly," *Washington Post*, December 9, 2014.

COPS Office. "Regional Community Policing Institutes," 2015, http://www.cops.usdoj.gov/Default.asp?Item=115.

Davey, Monica, and Tanzina Vega. "Chaos in Ferguson Is Fueled by Tangle of Leadership," *New York Times*, August 20, 2014.

Dempsey, John, and Linda Forst. *Police.* Clifton Park, NY: Delmar, Cengage Learning, 2013.

Department of Defense. "Crisis Communications Strategies: Case Studies, Jack in the Box," 2015, http://www.ou.edu/deptcomm/dodjcc/groups/02C2/Jack%20in%20the%20Box.htm.

Department of Justice. *Department of Justice Report Regarding the Criminal Investigation into the Shooting Death of Michael Brown by Ferguson, Missouri Police Officer Darren Wilson*, March 4, 2015.

Department of Justice, Civil Rights Division. *Investigation of the Ferguson Police Department*, March 15, 2015.

Drug Policy Alliance. "The Drug War, Mass Incarceration and Race," n.d., http://www.drugpolicy.org/resource/drug-war-mass-incarceration-and-race.

Duke, Alan. "Ex-Los Angeles Police Chief Dies," CNN, April 16, 2010, http://www.cnn.com/2010/US/04/16/obit.gates/.

Eck, John, and Robin Engel. *Effectiveness vs. Equity in Policing: Is a Tradeoff Inevitable?* Ideas in American Policing no. 18. Washington, DC: Police Foundation, 2015.

Eggers, William D., and John O'Leary. "No Easy Answers: An Interview with James Q. Wilson," *Reason* (February 1995).

Eith, Christine, and Matthew R. Burose, "Contacts Between the Police and the Public, 2008," Bureau of Justice Statistics, NCJ 234599, Washington, DC, 2011.

Elias, Paul, and Greg Risling. "Oscar Grant Verdict: Oakland Riots after Johannes Mehserle Convicted of Involuntary Manslaughter," AP/ *Huffington Post*, July 9, 2010, http://www.huffingtonpost.com.

Ellsworth, Scott. "Tulsa Race Riot," *Encyclopedia of Oklahoma History and Culture*, n.d., http://www.okhistory.org/publications/enc/entry.php ?entry=TU013.

Fang, Marina. "Baltimore Mayor Apologizes for Calling Protesters 'Thugs,'" *Huffington Post*, April 29, 2015, http://www.huffingtonpost.com/.

Farrar, Tony. "SELF-Awareness to Being Watched and Socially Desirable Behavior: A Field Experiment on the Effect of Body Worn Cameras on Police Use of Force." Washington, DC: Police Foundation, 2013, http://www.policefoundation.org/.

Fatteross, John. "Advantages of Strong Brand Equity," *Hartford Business Owner's Playbook*, n.d., https://www.thehartford.com/business-playbook /in-depth/advantages-strong-brand-equity.

Flatrow, Nicole. "NYPD Stop and Frisk Lead to More Marijuana Arrests than Anything Else," ThinkProgress, May 24, 2013, http://thinkprogress .org/justice/2013/05/24/2057481/analysis-nypd-stop-and-frisks-lead-/.

Flexon, Jamie L., Arthur Lurigio, and Richard Greenleaf. "Exploring the Dimensions of Trust in the Police among Chicago Juveniles," *Journal of Criminal Justice*, 37 (2009), 180–89.

Follman, Mark. "Michael Brown's Mom Laid Flowers Where He Was Shot—and Police Crushed Them," *Mother Jones*, August 27, 2014, http://www.motherjones.com.

Force Science News. "1 Agency's Commitment to Changing Cop Culture," *Force Science News*, 283 (2015), http://www.forcescience.org.

Fox, Lauren. "There's a Huge Racial Gap in Trust of Police: Can Congress Fix It?" The Atlantic, December 8, 2014, http://www.theatlantic.com.

FoxNews.com. "Missouri Gov Calls for 'Vigorous Prosecution' of Ferguson Shooting Case," Fox News, August 19, 2014, http://www.foxnews.com /us/2014/08/20/missouri-gov-calls-for-vigorous-prosecution-ferguson -shooting-case.html.

Freelon, Kiratiana. "The #nmos14 started on Twitter, Organized on Facebook, and Looks to Connect People IRL tonight," *Washington Post*, August 14, 2014.

French, David. "The Numbers Are In—Black Lives Matter Are Wrong about the Police," *National Review*, December 29, 2015.

Friedersdorf, Connor. "How Police Unions and Arbitrators Keep Abusive Cops on the Streets," *The Atlantic*, December 2, 2014.

Gates, Henry Louis, Jr. "Thirteen Ways of Looking at a Black Man." In R. Kennedy (ed), *Race, Crime and the Law*. New York: Pantheon Books, 1997.

Geller, W., and G. Swanger. *Managing Innovation in Policing*. Washington, DC: Police Executive Research Forum, 1995.

Gladwell, Malcolm. *Tipping Point: How Little Things Can Make a Big Difference*. New York: Little, Brown, 2000.

GlobalNewsCentre.com. "Being Confronted by Officer Go F*ck Yourself in Ferguson," Global News Centre, December 7, 2014, http://www.global newscentre.com/_.

Goldman, Roger, and Steven Puro. "Revocation of Police Officer Certification: A Viable Remedy for Police Misconduct?" *Saint Louis University Law Journal*, 45 (2001), 541.

Goldstein, Dana. "Explaining the Great Crime Decline: From Aging to Gentrification to Prozac: 10 (Not Entirely Crazy) Theories," Marshall Project, November 24, 2014, https://www.themarshallproject.org/.

Goldstein, Diane. "Take It from a Cop: The Drug War Poisons Community Policing," Substance.com, August 21, 2014, http://www.substance .com/take-it-from-an-ex-cop-the-drug-war/.

Goldstein, Herman. *Problem Oriented Policing*. New York: McGraw-Hill, 1990.

Grasha, Kevin. "AG: Cincinnati Police a Nationwide Model," *Cincinnati Enquirer*, May 19, 2015, http://.cincinnati.com/.

Greenwald, Glenn. *Drug Decriminalization in Portugal: Lessons for Creating Fair and Successful Drug Policies*. Washington, DC: Cato Institute, 2009.

Hall, John. "Constitutional Constraints on the Use of Force," *FBI Law Enforcement Bulletin*, 61, no. 2 (1992), 22–31.

Hampson, Rick, Marisol Bello, and Kevin Johnson. "Nine Solutions to Fix Ferguson," *USA Today*, March 13, 2015.

Harris, David. "The Stories, the Statistics, and the Law: Why 'Driving While Black' Matters," *Minnesota Law Review*, 84, no. 2 (1999), 265–326.

Hartmann, Margaret. "National Guard Deployed after Chaotic, Violent Night in Ferguson," *New York Magazine*, August 18, 2014.

Harwell, Drew. "Obama's Drug Use Debated," CBS News, February 12, 2008, http://www.cbsnews.com/news/obamas-drug-use-debated/.

Heritage Foundation. "100,000 Cops on the Beat? Not Even If You Use New Math," Heritage Foundation, September 25, 2000, http://www.heritage.org/.

Hunt, Amber. "What DuBose's Rap Sheet Tells Us about Him and the Police," *Cincinnati Enquirer*, August 9, 2015.

International Association of Chiefs of Police. *Police Use of Force in America*, Gaithersburg, MD: IACP, 2001.

Jackman, Michael. "The Summer of '43," *Detroit Metro Times*, June 18, 2003, http://www.metrotimes.com/.

Jacobs, D., and R. O'Brien. "The Determinants of Deadly Force: A Structural Analysis of Police Violence," *American Journal of Sociology*, 103, no. 4 (1998), 837862.

Johns, Tommy. "Responding to Individuals with Mental Illness," unpublished paper written for the Southern Police Institute, 2001.

Johnson, Alan, and Catherine Candisky. "Heroin Feeds Record Number of Ohio Drug Deaths," *Columbus Dispatch*, May 1, 2015, www.dispatch .com/.

Jones, Jeffrey. "In U.S., Confidence in Police Lowest in 22 Years," Gallup, June 19, 2015, http://www.gallup.com/poll/183704/confidence-police -lowest-years.aspx.

Kane, John L. "Policy Is Not a Synonym for Justice." Chapter 5 in Bill Masters (ed.), *The New Prohibition: Voices of Dissent Challenge the Drug War*, St. Louis: Accurate Press, 2004.

Kaste, Martin. "Why Police Departments Have a Hard Time Recruiting Blacks," NPR, December 10, 2014, http://www.npr.org/.

Kaye, Kimberlee. "Black Panther Leader Trains with Police, Has a Change of Heart," *Legal Insurrection*, February 9, 2015, http://legalinsurrection.com /2015/02/black-panther-leader-trains-with-police-has-a-change-of-heart/.

Kelling, George L., and James Q. Wilson. "Broken Windows: The Police and Neighborhood Safety," *Atlantic Monthly*, 249, no. 3 (1982), 29–38.

Kelling, G., T. Pate, D. Dieckman, and C. Brown. "The Kansas City Preventive Patrol Experiment: A Technical Report," Police Foundation, Washington, DC, 1974.

Kennedy, R. *Race, Crime, and the Law*. New York: Pantheon Books, 1997.

Kindy, Kimberly, Marc Fisher, Julie Tate, and Jennifer Jenkins. "A Year of Reckoning: Police Fatally Shoot Nearly 1000," *Washington Post*, December 26, 2015.

Kindy, Kimberly, and Kelly Kimbriell. "Thousands Dead, Few Prosecuted," *Washington Post*, April 22, 2015.

Kinnard, Meg. "Is It Skill or Gambling? Poker Players Watch as SC Judge Considers Legality of Texas Hold 'Em," Fox News, January 29, 2009, http://www.foxnews.com/.

Lacey-Bordeaux, Emma. "Louisville Police Officer Helps 'Inspirational Woman' Finish 10k," CNN, March 23, 2015, http://www.cnn.com/police.

Leen, J., and S. Horwitz. "Armed and Unready: City Pays for Failure to Train Officers With Sophisticated Weapon," *Washington Post*, November 18, 1998, p. A-1.

Linder, Doug. "The Trials of Los Angeles Police Officers in Connection with the Beating of Rodney King," 2001.

Linderman, Juliet. "Baltimore Gets Bloodier as Arrests Drop Post Freddie Gray," Associated Press, May 28, 2015, http://www.seattletimes.com /nation-world/baltimore-gets-bloodier-as-arrests-drop-post-freddie-gray/.

Locke, H. G. "The Color of Law and the Issue of Color: Race and the Abuse of Police Power." In W. Geller and H. Toch (eds), *And Justice for All: Understanding and Controlling Police Abuse of Force*, Washington, DC: Police Executive Research Forum, 1995.

Lowery, Wesley, Kimberly Kindy, Keith L. Alexander. "Distraught People, Deadly Results," *Washington Post*, June 30, 2015.

MacDonald, Heather. "Excusing the Oakland Rioters: Looting Is Not a Form of Civil Rights Protest," *Weekly Standard*, 15, no. 42 (July 26, 2010).

MacDonald, Heather. "Safe Streets Ahead?" *City Journal*, 2013, http://www.city-journal.org/2013/special-issue_crime.html.

Maher, Sean. "Man Fatally Shot in Hayward Identified as Oscar Grant III's Best Friend," *Oakland Tribune*, July 31, 2011.

Major Cities Chiefs Association, Major County Sheriffs Association, and Federal Bureau of Investigation National Executive Institute. "Engagement-Based Policing: The What, How, and Why of Community Engagement," May 27, 2015, https://majorcitieschiefs.com/.

Males, Mike, and Lizzie Buchen. "Reforming Marijuana Laws. What Approach Best Reduces the Harms of Criminalization," Center on Juvenile and Criminal Justice, September 24, 2014, http://www.cjcj.org/news/8200.

Marcus, Ruth. "Policing by Fleecing in Ferguson and Beyond," *Washington Post*, March 6, 2014, https://www.washingtonpost.

Marijuana Policies of Ohio Task Force. "Marijuana and Ohio: Past, Present, Potential," Cincinnati, OH, June, 2015, http://www.cincinnati.com/.

Mazerolle, Lorraine, Sarah Bennett, Jacqueline Davis, Elise Sargeant, and Matthew Manning. *Legitimacy in Policing: A Systematic Review*. Campbell Collection Library of Systematic Reviews no. 9, Oslo, Norway: Campbell Collaboration, 2013a.

Mazerolle, Lorraine, Sarah Bennett, Jacqueline Davis, Elise Sargeant, and Matthew Manning. *Legitimacy in Policing*. Crime Prevention Research Review no. 10, Washington, DC: US Department of Justice, Office of Community Oriented Policing Services, 2013b.

McCabe, David. "Maryland Governor Glad Baltimore Mayor 'Finally' Requested State Aid," *The Hill*, April 27, 2015, http://thehill.com/.

McCarthy, Anna. "Demo over BART Shooting Turns Violent," *510 Report*, January 8, 2009, http://510report.org/.

McClam, Errin, and Pete Williams. "Chattanooga Shooting: Attacker Had Three Guns, Authorities Say," NBCNews.com, July 17, 2015, http://www.nbcnews.com/storyline/chattanooga-shooting/chattanooga-shooting-attacker-had-least-three-guns-authorities-say-n394046.

Mekhennet, Souad. "Even the Islamists of ISIS Are Obsessing over Ferguson," *Washington Post*, August 21, 2014.

Meshanko, Paul. *The Respect Effect*. New York: McGraw-Hill, 2013.

Meyer, Greg. "Brutal by Default: The Police Need More Humane Ways to Subdue Resisting Suspects," *Los Angeles Daily Journal*, August 19, 1993.

Meyer, Greg. "Finding a Safe Way to Subdue Violent Suspects: The 'Chokehold' Ban Merits Rational Reconsideration," *Los Angeles Times*, June 14, 1994.

Miller, Michael E. "Taser Use and the Use-of-Force Continuum: Examining the Effect of Policy Change," *Police Chief Magazine*, September 2010.

Mueller, Aaron. "Gun Violence Declines in Kalamazoo Neighborhood One Year after 13-Year-Old Killed," *Kalamazoo Gazette*, May 23, 2015.

Musto, David. *The American Disease*. New York: Oxford University Press, 1987.

NAMI (National Alliance on Mental Illness). "CIT Toolkit, CIT Facts," 2015, http://www2.nami.org/Content/ContentGroups/Policy/CIT/CIT_Facts_.

National Advisory Commission on Civil Disorder. "Summary Report," Eisenhower Foundation, 1967, http://www.eisenhowerfoundation.org/docs/kerner.pdf.

New York Civil Liberties Union. "Analysis Finds Racial Disparities in NYPD Stop and Frisk Program: Links Tactic to Soaring Marijuana Arrest Rates," NCLU, May 22, 2013, http://www.nyclu.org/news/analysis-finds-racial-disparities-ineffectiveness-nypd-stop-and-frisk-program-links-tactic-to soaring marijuana arrest rates.

New York State Division of Criminal Justice Service. "SWAT Operator Equivalency Course Certification," n.d., http://www.nytacticalexpo.com/files/SWAT%20Operator%20Equiv%20Application%20Jan%202013.pdf.

New York State Governor's Press Office. "Governor Cuomo Signs Executive Order Appointing NYS Attorney General as Special Prosecutor in Cases Where Law Enforcement Officers Are Involved in Deaths of Civilians," July 9, 2015, https://www.governor.ny.gov/news/governor-cuomo-signs-executive-order-appointing-nys-attorney-general-special-prosecutor-cases.

New York Times Editorial Board. "Racial Discrimination in Stop-and-Frisk," *New York Times*, August 12, 2013, http://www.nytimes.com/.

Nightengale, Bob. "MLB Making Inroads to Attract African Americans," *USA Today Sports*, April 15, 2015, http://www.usatoday.com/.

NORML.org. "Marijuana Decriminalization and Its Impact on Use," n.d., http://norml.org/aboutmarijuana/item/marijuana-decriminalization-its-impact-on-use-2.

Ohio State Bar Association. "Consensual Encounters," n.d., https://www.ohiobar.org/ForPublic/Resources/LawYouCanUse/Pages/LawYouCanUse-702.aspx.

Oklahoma Commission to Study the Tulsa Race Riot of 1921. "Tulsa Race Riot of 1921," February 2001, http://www.okhistory.org/research/forms/freport.pdf.

O'Neil, Julie. "New Police Weapon to Hit Tri-State Streets," WCPO-TV, July 4, 2011, http://www.wcpo.com/news/new-police-weapon-to-hit-tri-state-streets.

Ortiz, Erik. "Freddie Gray: From Baltimore Arrest to Protest, a Timeline of the Case," NBC News, May 1, 2015, http://www.nbcnews.com/.

O'Toole, Mike. "Five Steps to Building Brand Equity for the Small Business," *Marketing Professional*, 2008, http://www.marketingprofs.com/8/building-brand-equity-for-small-businesses-otoole.asp#ixzz3fv2SqrNN.

PBS. "American Experience: The Zoot Suit Riots of 1943," n.d., http://www
.pbs.org/.

Peralta, Eyder. "Timeline: What We Know about the Freddie Gray Arrest,"
NPR, May 1, 2015, http://www.npr.org/.

Perez, D. W., and W. Ker Muir. "Administrative Review of Alleged Police
Brutality." In W. Geller and H. Toch (eds), *And Justice for All:
Understanding and Controlling Police Abuses of Force*, Washington,
DC: PERF, 1995.

Perl, Peter. "Race Riot of 1919 Gave Glimpse of Future Struggles," *Washington
Post*, March 1, 1999, p. A1.

Pintado-Vertner, Ryan, and Jeff Chang. "The War on Youth," *Colorlines* 2,
no. 4. (1999–2000).

Pitcher, James. "Feds Seize $11,000 from Student for Pot Smell," *Cincinnati
Enquirer*, June 1, 2015, p. 11a.

Postrell, Virginia. "The Consequences of the 1960s Riots Come into View,"
New York Times, December 20, 2004, http://www.nytimes.com/.

Prendergrast, Jane. "NAACP Applauded Cops' Help," Cincinnati.com, July
22, 2008, http://archive.cincinnati.com/article/20080722/NEWS01
/307220099/NAACP-applauded.

President's Commission on Law Enforcement and Justice. "The Challenge of
Crime in a Free Society," March 1968, https://www.ncjrs.gov/pdffiles1
/nij/42.pdf.

President's Task Force on 21st Century Policing, *Final Report of the
President's Task Force on 21st Century Policing*. Washington, DC:
Office of Community Oriented Policing Services, May, 2015.

Purnick, Joyce. "Policing Police Proves Hard for Civilians," *New York
Times*, December 5, 1996, http://www.nytimes.com/.

Rahr, Sue. "Transforming the Culture of Policing from Warriors to Guardians
in Washington State," *International Association of Directors of Law
Enforcement Standards and Training Newsletter*, 25, no. 4 (2014).

Rahr, Sue and Stephen K. Rice. *From Warriors to Guardians: Recommitting
American Police Culture to Democratic Ideals*. New Perspectives in
Policing Bulletin, Washington, DC: U.S. Department of Justice,
National Institute of Justice, 2015. NCJ 248654.

Rahtz, Howard. *Community Policing: A Handbook for Beat Cops and
Supervisors*. Boulder: Lynne Rienner Publishers, 2001.

Rahtz, Howard. *Understanding Police Use of Force*. Boulder: Lynne Rienner
Publishers, 2003.

Rahtz, Howard. *Drugs, Crime and Violence: From Trafficking to Treatment*.
Lanham, MD: Hamilton Books, 2012.

Ray, Raphael. *Cash Crop: An American Dream*. Caspar, CA: Ridge Times
Press, 1985.

Reaves, Brian. "Census of State and Local Police Departments, 2008,"
Department of Justice, Bureau of Justice Statistics, 2011, http://www.bjs
.gov/content/pub/pdf/csllea08.pdf.

Ridgeway, Greg. "Analysis of Racial Disparities in the New York Police Department's Stop, Question, and Frisk Practices," RAND Corporation, Santa Monica, CA, 2007, http://www.rand.org/pubs/technical_reports /TR534.

Robbe, Hindrick, and James O'Hanlon. "Marijuana, Alcohol and Actual Driving Performance," No. HS 808,939, National Highway Traffic Safety Administration. Washington, DC, 1999.

Robinson, Matthew B., and Renee G. Scherlen. *Lies, Damned Lies, and Drug War Statistics: A Critical Analysis of Claims Made by the Office of National Drug Control Policy.* Albany: State University of New York Press, 2007.

Rucker, Walter C., and James N. Upton. *Encyclopedia of American Race Riots, Volume 1.* Westport, CT: Greenwood Publishers, 2006.

Sack, Kevin, and Megan Thee-Brenan. "Poll Finds Most in U.S. Hold Dim View of Race Relations," *New York Times,* July 24, 2015, http://www .nytimes.com/.

Salter, Jim, and Alicia Caldwell. "Cheap, Ultra-potent Heroin Is Causing Rise in Deaths," Associated Press, May 24, 2010, http://www.salon .com/.

Schuppe, Jon. "Science of Strangers Military Research Could Boost Cops' People Skills," NBC News, October 22, 2014, http://www.nbcnews.com /news/us-news/science-strangers-military-research-could-boost-cops -people-skills-n230951.

Shackford, Scott. "Forfeiture Reform," *Reason,* 47, no. 4 (2015), 9–10.

Sherman, L., D. Gottfredson, D. MacKenzie, J. Eck, P. Reuter, and S. A. Bushway. "Report to the United States Congress," University of Maryland, 1998, https://www.ncjrs.gov/works/index.htm.

Sherman, Lawrence, Catherine H. Milton, and Thomas Kelly. *Team Policing: Seven Case Studies.* Washington, DC: Police Foundation, 1973.

Sibilla, Nick. "Philadelphia Earns Millions by Seizing Cash and Homes from People Never Charged with a Crime," *Forbes,* August 26, 2014, http://www.forbes.com/sites/instituteforjustice/2014/08/26/philadelphia -civil-forfeiture-class-action-lawsuit/.

Simon, Richard. "Colorful Figure Polarized Opinion," *Los Angeles Times,* June 6, 1998, http://articles.latimes.com/1998/jun/06/news/mn-57088.

Skogan, W. "Asymmetry in the Impact of Encounters with Police," *Policing and Society,* 16 (2006), 99–126.

Skolnick, J. H., and J. J. Fyfe. *Above the Law: Police and Excessive Use of Force.* New York: Free Press, 1993.

Smiley, Travis. "It's a Dignity Thing—Democracy Is Threatened by Racism and Poverty," *Time* Magazine, May 11, 2015.

Stroud, Matt. "How Can a Cop Mistake His Gun for a Taser," *Bloomberg News,* April 29, 2015, http://www.bloomberg.com/.

Stahl, Kenneth. "The Great Rebellion," n.d., http://www.detroits-great
-rebellion.com/.

Stamper, Norm. "Nothing Works in Ferguson: Here's How to Fix a Police
Force—And Punish Cops," *Guardian*, August 19, 2014, http://www
.theguardian.com/commentisfree/2014/aug/19/ferguson-police-force
-punish-cops.

Stillman, Sarah. "SWAT Team Nation," *New Yorker*, August 8, 2013,
http://www.newyorker.com/news/daily-comment/swat-team-nation.

St. Martin, Victoria. "45 Years after Riots Tore at Heart of Newark, City
Recalls 5 Days of Mayhem," *Star-Ledger*, July 15, 2012, www.nj.com/.

Stockey, Grif. "Elaine Massacre," *Encyclopedia of Arkansas History and
Culture*, Butler Center for Arkansas Studies, n.d., http://www.encyclopedia
ofarkansas.net/encyclopedia/entry-detail.aspx?entryID=1102.

Terkel, Amanda. "Police Officer on Video Calling Michael Brown Protesters
'F***ing Animals,'" *Huffington Post*, August 12, 2014, http://www
.huffingtonpost.com/.

The Local. "German Journalists Arrested in Ferguson," August 19, 2014,
http://www.thelocal.de.

Trimel, Suzanne. "Amnesty International Urges Stricter Limits on Police
Taser Use as U.S. Death Toll Reaches 500," Amnesty USA, February
15, 2012, http://www.amnestyusa.org/news/press-releases/amnesty
-international-urges-stricter-limits-on-police-taser-use-as-us-death-toll
-reaches-500.

Tweh, Bowdeye. "Russell Simmons–Backed Initiative Donates $25K to
Cincy Nonprofit," *Cincinnati Enquirer*, August 7, 2015.

Tybout, Alice M., and Michelle Roehm. "Let the Response Fit the Scandal,"
Harvard Business Review, December 2009, https://hbr.org/.

US Sentencing Commission. "Fifteen Years of Guidelines Sentencing,"
November 2004, http://www.ussc.gov/research-and-publications
/research-projects-and-surveys/miscellaneous/fifteen-years-guidelines
-sentencing.

Varghese, Johnlee. "Michael Brown Shooting: Tibetan Monks Join Ferguson
Protesters," *International Business Times*, August 18, 2014, http://www
.ibtimes.

Wartman, Scott. "Kids, Cops Find Common Ground on Football Field,"
Cincinnati Enquirer, August 7, 2015.

West, Allen. "The Dirty Little Secret No One Wants to Admit about
Baltimore," Allenbwest.com, April 29, 2015, http://allenbwest.com
/2015/04/the-dirty-little-secret-no-one-wants-to-admit-about-baltimore/.

Westphal, Lonnie. "The In-Car Camera: Value and Impact," *Police Chief
Magazine*, November 9, 2004.

White, M. D. "Controlling Police Decisions to Use Deadly Force: Reexamining
the Importance of Administrative Policy," *Crime & Delinquency*, 47, no. 1
(2001), 131–151.

Williams, Clarence, and Peter Herman. "Lanier Eliminates Many Plainclothes Drug Units to Focus on Top Dealers," *Washington Post*, June 12, 2015.

Williams, Jason. "UC Chief 'Horrified' by Tickets Given to Black People," *Cincinnati Enquirer*, August 11, 2015, http://www.cincinnati.com/.

Wing, Nick. "Marijuana Prohibition Was Racist from the Start: Not Much Has Changed," *Huffington Post*, January 14, 2014, http://www.huffingtonpost.com.

WLWT-TV. "UC President, CPD Chief Ask Judges to 'Send Message' to Criminals," WLWT, December 5, 2013, http://www.wlwt.com/news/local-news/cincinnati/uc-president-cpd-chief-ask-judges-to-send-message-to-criminals/23302898.

Woolverton, Paul. "Taser Use Restricted in Five States," *Fayetteville Observer*, January 15, 2016, http://www.policeone.com/.

WXIX-TV. "7 Arrested in Fountain Square Melee," WXIX, July 6, 2015, http://www.fox19.com/story/29476313/officers-respond-to-unruly-crowd-at-fountain-square.

Young, Virginia. "Legislature Vows to Find Out Why National Guard Didn't Protect Ferguson Businesses," *St. Louis Post-Dispatch*, December 11, 2014, http://www.stltoday.com.

Index

About the Book

Reflected almost daily in headlines, the enormous rift between the police and the communities they serve—especially African American communities—remains one of the major challenges facing the United States. And race-related riots continue to be a violent manifestation of that rift. Can this dismal state of affairs be changed? Can the distrust between black citizens and the police ever be transformed into mutual respect?

Howard Rahtz addresses this issue, first tracing the history of race riots in the US and then drawing on both the lessons of that history and his own first-hand experience to offer a realistic approach for developing and maintaining a police force that is a true community partner.

Howard Rahtz served for nearly two decades with the Cincinnati Police Department, retiring in 2007 as commander of the Vice Control Unit. He currently teaches at police academies in the area and speaks nationally on police reform. He is the author of *Community Policing: A Handbook* and *Understanding Police Use of Force*.